CODE ONE

JUST CODEY

PHILIP RENOUD

ARCHWAY
PUBLISHING

Archway Publishing books may be ordered through booksellers or by contacting:

Archway Publishing
1663 Liberty Drive
Bloomington, IN 47403
www.archwaypublishing.com
844-669-3957

Scripture taken from the King James Version of the Bible.

ISBN: 978-1-4808-9753-3 (sc)
ISBN: 978-1-4808-9751-9 (hc)
ISBN: 978-1-4808-9752-6 (e)

Library of Congress Control Number: 2020925024

Print information available on the last page.

Archway Publishing rev. date: 12/17/2020

LEATHER

Writing in Hell: Mostly about how broken the "whole" is, trying to appreciate how the sum is greater than the parts. Alcohol and Cats: The enemy within. All kinds of deviance; traps, revenge, boogeyman and entirely false. Going On: We all agree it needs a veil, but that can't be so thick that evil can exist behind it. This is vain because it's immature.

The man never spoke to Nakita but kept a very persistent dialogue with her memory. It wasn't fair to the new world to drag wickedness into Penelope's life, so he kept Nakita quiet as much as possible. Yet, the man found joy in comparing the two women. The reality of man's progress over thousands of years was totally lost to Nakita and it was comforting to think Penelope was as naive to her Father. She frustrated the man because she had so much help from someone so far away and there was no substitute, so there was no one to appeal to and no appeal to her autonomy, even when she made mistakes - he almost hoped Penelope would go too far to give the man a fighting chance at leading her.

Nakita, he imagined, would cut - meaning intercession - like the fixer, and save the man from laboring against impossible tasks. He was never sure the spirit that saves him is holy - disgrace had a wicked taste he couldn't easily forget. He kept faith in a spirit that would intercede where there was only grace. Now that the man had real distance (of space) from Nakita he imagined her as the agent of disgrace - the bane of his Savior.

He let his hair grow over his eyes and dreamed of a simpler life more in his control - he disbelieved Penelope was growing the same direction along the fault-lines of Nakita.

Penelope was aware of the man's natural path towards a home and family and that she was unable to provide that for him. She knew not the Father of the man and believed he was willing to die in vain if she wasn't clear enough on this point. So she said,

"Tell me what you want from me so I can serve you better."

He wasn't sure he heard her correctly, so he said, "I was only waiting for you."

The man realized how that sounds too late, and blushed. The cross was so close, before, that he didn't imagine service beyond goodness.

"My plan," he said, "is to become a service, as you are to me, but I have only enough to serve myself."

The man should find happiness pursuing that, but he was still reconciling his new eternal life with the anarchy he narrowly avoided.

"I have suspicions that I'll have to suffer to become what you are to me," the man confessed.

So they waited; she made tea while he looked out of the window.

"To the extent that we're not helping each other there must be prayers we haven't shared."

"Up there is pretty arbitrary - flying like this."

"What I mean is there must be someone else (Jesus) who is conflicted by serving two masters."

"You mean our fathers should meet?"

"No - I mean I want to know what we don't pray together."

Game Over: The end is a surprise - even though it was expected - because it was harder or softer than expected. Found Jesus and the Devil inside. They need an intervention but they're deaf to Him. Saint Francis of Assisi.

"Even as you serve me and I serve myself we have secrets - I do know this much."

They shared tea for a very long time, somewhat comforted by this mystery. The man didn't notice he had begun confusing Penelope with Nakita; he thought her friends were too far - that he would never be close to the world in which she prayed. She was careful not to trespass on the man's secrets, but as she had interceded so far, her world did trespass - she didn't know how far her life was affecting her companion. In this way she had something in common with Nakita - *Ozery* had to be without boundaries. They were subject to a mysterious will that knew the secrets they kept.

The Big Guy had plans that ended in disgrace but he wasn't the only one - Nakita had plans too. Now that the Big Guy was just a memory she found herself in a dilemma - not sure if she should start over or wait for the business of faith to take hold or take action. She didn't want things to change but she was the only person left with enough autonomy to speak against the silence of fear just below the surface of the changes. She spurned the idea that salvation was there all along and that the crew waited until now - until some disgrace - to seek it sincerely. She sat with her head bent, staring at a tatoo of an anchor, when the thought occurred to her that she would demonstrate the hypocrisy she felt on the ship.

Being the only woman in the crew, she was tempted to throw her fondness at lost causes, madly, and sacrifice her well earned respect with the crew for the bitterness she felt towards them.

Meanwhile, the crew began to realize she wasn't helping when their prayers fell on deaf ears - they weren't sure at first, but it became clear she was not participating in the changes.

They began to refer to her as "the snag" and one man reflected on the exile of the fixer, who had permanently retired to the "pit" where all of *the machine* was. In a lot of ways they had both, Nakita and the Fixer, isolated themselves and the one man remembered it wasn't the Fixer's choice. At least, it seemed that way, because he rebelled from there against the tyranny of sending the Gimp first, who would have been in danger by himself.

The one man supposed that Nakita had noble reasons for her isolation, despite the impatience of the other crew members with her disconfirmation - her sacrifice seemed tasteful so far to him. He wondered how long she would exile herself before leaving and then worried that she may burn the crew before that.

So the worst came to pass, as a historic example of the complexity of what others accepted as blunt. She took that one man as a father of a child she didn't want to begin with - had a baby in cold blood. This damnation made others physically sick and she had no remorse.

"How did you find me?" the man who wore a red coat enquired, when a communication droid finally found him. The answer was magic - she didn't know what she was doing - very much like how he had escaped in his pod: the Fixer helped.

Penelope was sweating while she waited for the man - neither of them anticipated an awkward loose end like this - as if he was the father. She was careful to let this pass as suddenly as it began - but she wasn't sure how much history was involved. As soon as it became apparent that she was a single mother she knew she would have to intercede. She balked at the idea of undoing months of freedom and the danger she felt towards the other ship, just to find a broken family ... Nakita was barking up the wrong tree.

"Go home," she messaged clearly.

Nakita had been dwelling on a separate idea and confused the message with judgement - she quoth,

"Judge not, lest ye be judged."

The princess is sick. Deafness triggers. Troubled Customer: "Touch me," "I don't bite." "Because you can't hear me, let me get my supervisor."

"You mistake the action for judgement," Penelope replied dryly and continued, "how I judge waste is between me and my computer - it's sad that you think I judge people."

The chains are free - if you want to be the example then hold yourself to your law and if you live through it then judge others by it that they may profit from it.

"One more thing - I'm not trying to insult you - it's just that sweetness is sacred to me and I'm protecting the man from anything that threatens it, so use that."

Tugging Clippers. The enemy came from an arbitrary distance - all the way to the front lines - and that's where the enemy came in.

The Fixer knew the location of Penelope and the man, based on the communication droid, while Nakita lost interest entirely. She compromised with the crew to find her parents after exhausting her rebellion - a bitterness she couldn't exactly place. The father, Cody, was just beginning his descent and failed to understand how close Nakita was to not surrendering herself to a more humble life - he was hypnotized by ambition that largely exceeded a misadventure after a domestic life.

He overheard, from a corridor, crew talking openly about a cache left over from a failed mission. The company responsible still had a claim to it but had left it unguarded for years, based on its net value. They were discussing ideas to make it cost-effective, to contract themselves, to secure it.

Cody knew that he could save Nakita from a simple life and have something left over to invest this way, but he wouldn't compromise with the crew - that wasn't worth the passion he harbored.

Colonize something already! See Hudson Bay Company. If the space walker doesn't want to land then why do they go back up? More than anything, "up" is "out;" yet there is something unnatural about doing that often. Arabian Nights, Henson's Monoplane, and Delta's Dinghey - the pod. "Enjoy with [Him] amazement at how teamwork and dedication can manage the impossible." - Hinners, NASA, Viking. Someplace between Penelope and Cody there is a Delta, a Jesus Crew, but Cody needs Nakita's help. To the darkness, "I'll try to understand you if you try to understand me." - Muslim Child, Khan, R.

So Cody gathered as much information as he could and left the ship with Nakita and their child on a small transport the crew had used to ferry people and materials because by this time it had lost its value in re-entries.

"Flawless," he said, looking at the rust from sweat dew. That didn't stop him - he brushed off what kept things from working right and vacuumed it up so it wouldn't get in the food.

"You don't have to do this," she disdained.

"Please don't change your mind right now - I'm not done."

"How do I turn this thing on?"

"Let me do it - you have to do it in the right order."

So he did: he turned the main power on and found the checklist. Trying to remember where everything was, he frittered about humming awkwardly. He found the stabilizer - turned that on; then he found the navigation - turned that on; finally, he found the drive, followed the checklist, and waited to see if there was anything he forgot.

"Let's go - the crew knows this works - it's reliable."

So they did, knowing a child and mother did not belong with the others. They pulled out a few days away from Nakita's homeworld and waited for a sign that they were expected.

When someone is guilty of being obedient to sin then they need to be rebuked.

Ultimately, the sick want to get better, but it's the devil to do that the right way. That's the cold reason behind communications and leadership: to find the authority on the sin and assume the role. It was faith that kept me open to seek the end of sin rather than let sin exhaust me. (#Socrates'Trial)

I have witnessed the alternative, despite the fair weather and shelter of America. These are men and women who can't be honest, and don't have to be honest, so they get drunk on absurdity.

"I don't get angry when my mom smokes pot." (Sublime)

Now, there are two ways of looking at this: Adam and Eve, but this question arises, "Should I know?"

Here's the Red Pill:

Bitches sting; that "now" was "relax, take a deep breath," because your problem is you let the enemy passed the front line, like they're staff.

The enemy is not staff, it's distortion: lies. That's why we're so explicit about righteousness - to do it right. We have to go down with the Titanic to save bitches from their insanity.

The mission is to suss-out the problem and nurture sustainability; however, the Titanic is closed. The way into the Titanic is a weird mystery.

Jesus, that's His name! (aka. Immanuel, Jehova, Yaweh, etc.)

To make things easier, there is a Blue Pill: it's to resurrect the Titanic in an imaginary workshop, in a work of fiction, called, **Dead on the Island.**

It's delightful, but, it's anecdotal - food for thought.

It's all in Heaven: the Titanic fell as an old space transport converted into a stork of an escape boat. C.P.S. had to search it before the family could be reunited when out of nowhere a ghost steals the spotlight.

The babies momma is always getting so much heat from her father that she gets mercy in the form of ritualizing the ghost (to bring them) to help her soul navigate her family with respect to inviting people (to her family.)

It was outside her character to crystallize but she'll do it to rebuke snares at borders.

The enemy wanted the babies momma to surrender the child, so the enemy got a veil, while underwriters nurtured it, so that she wouldn't entertain the poison.

The end of the "blue pill" is when we remember specific individuals who suffer from mental illness and keep them in your prayers.

The babies momma is one of those people: Loki, which is Heaven's Fire.

The black-sheep side of things is about how they know the Anti-Christ and don't want to help the Anti-Christ: before the delightful presence of the Holy Spirit is penetrating, completely.

It's all forgiveness (at death.)

Because one God serves many people God reaps the service of many.

That's his name, again; Jesus is the way that service is teleological - putting Humans and Earth at the top of the visible and invisible Universe, in an inconsumable fire of a world without end.

Irony seems to take all that away so I make a strong distinction between these two types of smoke: marijuana and cigarettes because marijuana has a way of holding my attention while cigarettes distract me.

Looking around at the other animals (and expecting aliens) I have to admit dogs are distracting in a very intrusive way. In the spirit of mental health I think it's very important to be aware of negative behavior rather than be its slave.

Relax now, the Heaven Fire is delivering good news, because the Lord at hand is gloriously revealing the Love of God (it's not a fight!)

My own private story is from High School: straight from Absurdistan, like Yin and Yang, a girl from the next county south of mine moved in my senior year and was a desperate character for the *good college,* while mired in nonsense, and I got sucked into her fantasy! She was born yesterday and studied like her life depended on it. The amnesia was roses - absurdity showed - it all went out with pine. The studying was after her mom … while her dad was a teacher. The darkness was generally away from nonsense but the stress broke our relationship. (#TitsUp)

"What is your occupation?"

It's so hard to answer that question! She ought to be a homemaker but she got involved in wickedness, and the baby came out of that to encourage her to focus on family, but she is rude to the baby.

The incentive to respect the baby is merit.

"Then what is the highest level of education?"

Because she is frequently tempted by wickedness she can't achieve any success, and her home planet won't accept failure to nurture children, so,

"Then your family needs to be here to accept guardianship," the guard said as he turned to look at Cody, the babies daddy. Cody said nothing and He turned back to Nakita.

The wickedness is a curse of dishonor; when dishonor wins it is very similar to surrendering the passion I had for Nakita.

1. Prevention: "Only be thou strong and very courageous, that thou mayest observe to do according to the law, which Moses my servant has commanded thee: turn not from it ..." Joshua 1:6-7
2. Trust: the enemy is little and it's a mystery what happens to them when their inferiority is tested and found lacking.
3. Grace: "for I am persuaded, that neither death, nor life, nor angels, nor principalities, nor powers, nor things present, nor things to come, nor height, nor depth, nor any other creature, shall be able to separate us from the Love of God, which is in Christ Jesus our Lord."

I chose bitterness at first, but I decided that was her fault, so I went the other way.

1. Sugar: "A false balance is abomination to the Lord: but a just weight is His delight." Proverbs 11:1
2. Lambs: "He that is slow to anger is better than the mighty; and he that ruleth his spirit than he that taketh a city." Proverbs 16:32

I struggled with laziness, because it was watching weakness evolve into strength, and it corrupted the sweetness of leisure.

1. Messenger: "if thou be surety for thy friend, [yet] if thou hast stricken thy hand with a stranger, thou art snared ... thou art taken with the words of thy mouth." Proverbs 6:1-2
2. Judgement: "He becometh poor that dealeth with a slack hand: but the hand of the diligent maketh rich." Proverbs 10:4
3. Virtue: "Let me be an instrument of your peace ... for it is in giving we receive." Prayer of St. Francis

Courage, in the Life of Jesus, is like a rose: it has all the transforming power of nurturing, combined with sacrifice and suffering.

The Agony in the Garden is symbolic of the sacrifice sinners make to demonstrate courage in darkness - Jesus in Hell.

In Daniel and Saints there are similar trials that amount to David and Goliath.

For women it's to Mary, Mother of Mercy, our Life our Sweetness and our Hope. Eve is the fight to reconcile mystery as sweetness and hope rather than poison.

My Bible details the prophesies of the fight that Jesus has in the anarchy of sacrifice, and David's fight with Goliath is in the Old Testament; *these epitomes of darkness* reveal the courage these men engender through Faith - trust in God.

If that fight is hard for Mary then is it just as hard for the next mother?

I know Holy women who fell for temptation.

I know that temptation makes these fights worse; that is poison at courage. The rebuking of Eve is to do this: quest for Love's superiority, by putting on *the hope* for the courage of Man.

The ultimate point is that Nakita is the secret burden of Holy women and Cody is retiring in a peace unstained by suffering and sacrifice.

In Eve's disbelief, Adam put love so that she would learn to choose to hope for courage rather than choose to be obedient to sin.

The fall of Man is to find love in courage.

Eve is impatient for eternal life.

The law of God came first, through the prophets, and the Jews have been struggling to conform to it ever since … it's a problem how miserably Eve fails to keep life (babies died.)

She slaves the law to sacrifice herself for the future that despises her failure to get what she wants after this arbitrarily long life of hers.

Jesus breathed life into her as if she lost Adam.

Everything is supposed to be honkey-doory, now that Jesus' Life is very explicitly in everything.

What happened to Adam's love of courage?

There are two options, in my mind:

1. Help Eve end sin (come out.)
2. Socrates (play dead.)

There is a small chance Nakitas father is Socrates, reflecting civil-war, and it's easy to forget Jesus is in that fight (here!)

The parents have their own dead island, but they're sick: they're role models that fail to reach a wellness that parents want to share with children and no one knows why.

I have to go back in time to discover the nature of Nakita's parents - it helps that they are Heritage-buffs who nothing much changes for.

(All of these people are lost in lies they blame Eve for.)

As far as Cody is concerned, the family acts like a volatile rabbit.

The Father has to help himself to get out of negative habits and nurture positive behavior.

"In thee have they discovered their father's' nakedness …"

In despair, gentiles resist the world they were born into, yet they are sweethearts who wait in an exile of darkness like Cody and Nakita on the Island.

Before Israel fell into a darkness of detachment and self-degradation of decadent vanity and exuberant weakness, in hard times, God warned their father Abram. He failed to prevent it.

Abram was cursed for four-hundred years.

That up!

Welcome staff to check that my "Up" is sick.

This *Marie* is back to the Vatican from a sandbox dream of the Milky Way. **The dirt should be benign**, but Eve falls for the temptation that it isn't, and we'll find out Eve's plans for my future are negligible.

One last note, about this, is that it is negative to the enemy.

It is done in such a way that the enemy can't do it for themselves, which is what Socrates wants, and it is as clean as I want:

1. To witness the enemy make themselves harder to forgive.
2. That the enemy fails this way when their victim makes progress.

America is founded on this freedom to believe in yourself … before that, the church was founded on Jesus' Victory, and all of this is to heal the departure of Eve's sin, whether the mysterious little moth of a spirit chooses to be ethical or not.

The rush of intensity we know as Glory is powered by Jesus.

The portal is the Quest for Love's Superiority.

There is a great need for problem solving in this Quest because it's light in the dark. Cody epitomizes this discovery of wisdom to turn the disobedient - he is a child whose success in turning parents to Heaven is to witness secrets as a child. (See Native Spirit-Quest.)

I started playing Cody in Anarchy Online; the Subway, the Temple (level 70, ninja GTA, etc.) Foremans, and then I skipped the Inner Sanctum for Shadowlands. Hecklers, hecklers, and more hecklers, until Inferno Missions.

I skipped Jesus. (The Lord lived in Camelot.)

I PVP'd for ~4 years.

I made enemies outside the game because Camelot and Battlestation were a cross for them: trains, targeting, lag, magma, loot-right points, leadership & *organization* (Raid,) visibility, etc.

I performed better in open PVP than in Duels: my record was barely breaking even in duels and %200 in open PVP. I give credit to preparedness - that it is a skill.

How can anyone blame me for things outside of my control?

They didn't … like the outcome of engaging me. They were neutral between good and evil. Evil was usually the outcome.

Gentiles resemble them - the relationship is not clear, but they all favor leisure.

A rapid increase in heartbeat is the evil.

"Why am I jealous?" they ask.
"Did I do that?" I taunt.

I think they want Odyceus to be responsible for their jealousy because he's a legend.

What happens when you veil the legend? We're still getting results on that one.

The legend, Odysseus, was veiled with Cody - it was treated like sickness and death by slaves. (Someone took the original name and never used it.)

The father made slaves and freemen out of his children and the slaves got all the attention.

The gravity of Odysseus, behind Cody, is symbolized by slaves and capital punishment (the wars are done.)

The ultimatum against the gravity is Cody; the slaves believe changing Odysseus' name to Odyceus is literary murder.

A series of symbols juxtapose Cody's father with the dark lord. Just before the special tree there is a Mega-city where the dark lord is failing to sell vacuum cleaners, or whatever filth this anti-christ swears by. That's a nostalgia no one can tolerate - of solitude and ruins.

The Bear Patrol veils the pain, but there is a very strange effect of passing the dark lord.

The show dies there, with the limelight (camera.) It's like dawn - you've been falling asleep all day working out problems in your eternity when the tide turns and you want to be bad - for all the rudeness you tolerated - but that's just the special rock someone has already graffitied.

Cody will recall his own rose: the neighbor virgin who was never corrupted by the rock. Her name is River - she is the Pine - she made him whine and he put her on a pedestal of his heart.

She never accepted this and after seven years the fire died completely. It doesn't matter which planet he's on - River is always haunting him there, yet now she is crippled because she tortured him for years. River is now on the other side of the Bear Patrol, in the solitude and ruins of the dark lord.

The Blacksmith is not as far from the Dark Lord as the special rock leads one to believe, because it is a small world after all. The Blacksmiths Orchard has a guest house where mercy is a fight. The consequence is usually in everyone's favor, but there is a small chance it can turn into Fort Brag and die to its purpose of healing light, like crucifying Jesus.

This is Job - an honest man corrupted.

He accepted guardianship of slaves he can't keep and they rebelled with their severest intentions while he waits for that to turn into self-determination.

It got complicated when other people got involved: Loki was watching and, depending on the state of their soul, may react like the dark lord, Freemen, or slaves. It's no secret that slaves fight slaves.

The difficult part is that the dark lord also fights slaves - he has Eve's original sin in common with them, using privacy to harbor poison. If they are not defending poison they are fighting each other.

Slaves and Job lost hope in each other with a failed ultimatum. They became content with not helping and that escalated into the insanity of doing the exact opposite of their original intention of helping each other!

They went from, "Don't cross me," to "Hit me with your best shot," in a fit of rage. This is revealing how weak their intentions to help are. They got confused about how consequence works and doubt God because their slave habits broke like glass and changed beyond their control.

That over-reaction defines Nazis - starting a war at the worst time: depression.

They guessed wrong and that's what my family had done - several of them waited for me to fail, blaming me for their weakness and because that never happened, they over-reacted and haven't picked up all the pieces - that's why poverty is so ironic to me; they are poor in a way I will never be because they are still waiting for me to fail while I've been broke for the four years or so since I dropped out of college.

The Blacksmith and the dark lord are on two different sides of self-determination and the slaves have no self-determination (they just react, like Lizards, and it's not clear that the Blacksmiths hope for them is at all rigorous.)

It's a little clearer when you consider slaves as mentally ill - the argument that their brains are damaged by the wind. That fight is safe; in rare cases where the damage is unsafe America has Social Security for them. The emergency room s where that decision is made.

My crises were from biting off more than I could chew - so I had to quit a few jobs and drop out of college a few times - but it was safe.

The slaves have problems they can't quit or drop out from.

Anna's rose is the strictest interpretation of slave problems. The meaning is to measure the severity by how well one sleeps.

This is the perspective that problems only exist in darkness.

It's a rose because it all depends on the healing power of light.

I am on this side - I believe the Church, Library and other free, public resources are more than sufficient to address problems and it's a matter of willingness.

At the very bottom, A.A. reaches out, and it only gets better from there.

The example I have of the bottom is a fight over why they crucified Jesus. The truth is that His people over-reacted under Roman occupation. The lies are over-reaction to over-reaction that amounts to Eve - the neighbors used their fences and walls to harbor Eve. They want me to expose them and Cinderella's wicked step-family is the way to do it, but that ended when I discovered they blame me for their weakness. Like Cinderella, it wasn't enough to help the wicked - I had to leave.

It was about judging spirits and the wicked were dehumanizing great spirits. The people that are blind and deaf to the Lord's Spirit find doubt instead. That doubt flags them as a slave or a dark lord and everyone else is keeping a safe distance because the justice for this offense is the details of Titanic - a sudden realization that doubt is drowning - and the willingness to finally accept the help people are willing to give.

The Blacksmith's horse is judgement - the spirit guides you to apples and you give the apples to the horse. In this way there would be no question that you can judge a spirit and that the man is honorable, because the Orchard and the horse are in such good condition!

———————

River is a war as old as civilization and her aggression towards Cody, no matter which planet he is on, compelled me to end her.

Cody and Nakita's engagement is silver; they are still courting and everyone knows they're unskilled at living together. It's a vulnerable and precious private time of their lives and the phrase "Crash into me," expresses how severely distasteful River is. River is a sacrifice I can't endure - it's poison to fiancés. River corrupts civilization by sowing lust for money … this is why: she became a slave to poisoning fiancés.

She became a slave to poisoning fiancés because she couldn't stop it. My assertion is that it takes care of itself - it is its own punishment - and River will only stop when she becomes proof that the poison she can't stop stops automatically. She fell into the mechanics of the enemy so the only way out is to stop herself. Proof is too great a sacrifice and she binds herself to it. Trust isn't working - River trusts River, but not God! River doesn't know how severely wrong that is and she is seeking validation where she found this poison - she turned on herself and now she is obedient to the enemy (because she couldn't stop the enemy.)

I have accepted the impossibility of turning River away from the enemy - she willfully rejected my help with such severity that it is in no way reasonable to fight her or help her. I walk away from River with honest pleasure. She rejects my trust in God and that's impossibly more severe than simply rejecting me.

River can't be patient without sacrificing and fails to hide the sacrifice. Patience is soul - it's planting seeds and waiting for harvest. River destroys the harvest before it is done. She epitomizes evil and hides behind the enemy, pretending to be their victim, but that fear became a lie a long time ago when she became the worst evil she could become.

River exhausted mercy for the fear of becoming a victim, but it's a self fulfilling prophecy when the mercy ends. She became the enemy by fearing the enemy too severely - she over-reacted and crucified herself.

River won't accept her soul and her sacrifice got out of control when the justification was rejected. Her soul is what she needs to heal but she rejected that capacity when she rejected her soul.

My initial assertion is with Jesus: sacrifice is only for the enemy and it is this assertion where River is fighting Jesus and I. She rejects how critical this assertion is: "The wages of sin is death."

River is a slave of Eve and the point I make is simply that these are a sacrifice - they don't really reject that notion, but for all their confidence in it they can't seem to articulate it. The problem they have is fatherlessness - the means to understand anything other than sacrifice. They believe their sacrifice, being the enemy, can only be articulated at a cost, a sacrifice; that is why they reject their salvation. I have done what they could not.

In this modern age there is a similarity between computer literacy and fatherlessness. River expected to fail, and does fail, while I reflect on her.

The allegory I have of beating the dead - the living who accept failure - is Cinderella's success.

Cinderella's wicked step sister demonstrates this evil - she is aware of the spirit of their dead father and she is simply disobedient to the destiny their father wants for his children, for no reason, just to spite a man with no body. She does this by attempting to drive a wedge between Cinderella and her father.

Cinderella was succeeding because she was obedient and her wicked step sister was insane enough to expect that she could cripple her like Eve corrupted Adam. The whole allegory is about how the honorable - the obedient - succeed where evil fails. Evil assumes there is very little difference between good and evil, but I can't endure that, and here I have rejected that poison forever.

How far? This far. Slaves want a sign; slaves got a sign. They lived in a paradigm of sickness where certain behavior causes certain punishments and they don't want to be right, aren't right, and this is why. They rot and I'm tired of the smell.

This is not to say that consequence is broken - it is to say that sin is death and it is unjustifiable. Slaves have now died believing in the justification of sin. They thought they could cause sin, were wrong, and now they can only think they can make things better.

The nasty piece of work that rotting is rejects a slave's capacity to self-determine the love of God. They weren't hoping, they were thresholding sin and it took a sign, Jesus, to get them to want to change. They're numb to normal signs and the fire is that God had to send his only son to get them to want to change.

It's hard to understand why Jesus needs a veil, but my explanation is that his Salvation is tears. I have fictionalized the tears, to give hope to slaves, as River.

Slave tears were literary murder, but I promised everyone my characters are safe and this has just now been validated.

"Wherefore seeing that we also are compassed about with so great a cloud of witnesses, let us lay aside every weight, and the sin which doth so easily beset us, and let us run with patience the race that is set before us.

Looking unto Jesus [who] ... endured the cross, despising the shame ..." Hebrews 12 : 1-2

(For myself, I promised glory, but the devil fought my confidence. Now I have a victory in glory!)

The Dark Lord and River won't help others because they are ashamed by their failure to self-determine a victory in glory. That is the devil and by that death there is an eternal life for everyone else, through the cleansing fire that our glory is.

Doubt kept River down and the sick part is when Cody had sex with Nakita it changed River's mind - animating the long dead feelings that she repressed. It is very clear that River made poor decisions because doubt served her so well that she is still a virgin. She is unique like Mary - escaping outrageous misfortune. To be clear, I mean Gentiles are commonly unfortunate.

The interesting part is how dark that fortune is. River really benefits from doubt and she is in ironic, yet severe danger by violating her crippledness after it happened - she wants to turn back time and undo Nakita, but I won't. Adding regret to doubt will kill River instead. Long story short, the heart attack is temporary - the Dark Lord pulled out his defibrillator and got weird with her.

River didn't accept crippling because it handicapped her - which there is no recovery from. However, resurrection really got her attention.

Meanwhile, the computer that handles waste like River is converging on the ideal fuel for nuclear fusion. It's important to note that the computer prefers to save River but right now that is impossible.

The thing about heart attacks is that there is a narrow window and that suits River because she keeps running away from fights she started. I try to be reasonable with her about her parents but she is comfortable with her mother's sin: cheating, and that calls for a numbness that rejects her rights, like war. Wars turn into original sin and the benefit is to put everyone on a fair level. When that happens it is like a reality check and peace can be made, but before that no one was negotiating because we couldn't agree there was a problem, much less what the problem was.

I have terms for her parents to agree to and they are in no position to reject them. The concern is that they are monsters and they need to be rebuked before they can know how weak their position is. (They are incomprehensibly poor.)

Until the enemy surrenders, base-camp is here, in Revelation, and it's kind of the top. The enemy lost control, got raped, had a baby in their anarchy, rejects responsibility, and the law is waiting for them in the religion of the Rosary.

When we get tired and cry for our tradition we lose our capacity to be honest to a degree of calling out the enemy with threats of severe accidents.

We are polite coast people with a passion for babies. "My tears have fed me day and night while some have said, 'Where is your God?' But I recall, as my soul pours dry, the days of praise ..." [Psalm 42 (As the Deer Longs)]

My personal struggle is a missing sofa and clothes. The enemy is doing nothing to reconcile their struggle. They are mocking the humility of their victims. They don't fear the Lord and they don't take full responsibility, they pick and choose which evil they find pride in. They overreacted and I am revealing the part of the enemy they can't find pride in.

This is how self-interest is corrupted. The enemy feels entitled to pride like it is a matter of life and death. They have put futility in growth. I appreciate how much that needs a vale. It is a weirdness of feet, farts, cats, immaturity and insanity that belongs to River.

"She's dead; she's fucking dead," the dark lord frantically says to dispatch.

Now is a good time to confess that I am not trying to help sinners. I would baptize them in the middle of a circus with loud music and poison them with alcohol. I am fire and I shoot first. I accept, then, that less is more. I will hold the enemy's hand while they commit suicide.

The enemy belongs to me but their magic is no match for mine. They are slaves I can't keep because they are blinded by popularity. I am of

Abraham, who left Egypt because it was unstable and the covenant was broken. I led Nakita into the Enchanted Forest to find the Great Spirit because that had been lost.

I can't tell if Nakita is my friend or my enemy, but the worst case scenario is corn.

This is the eternity I choose rather than money. I like money, but I hate the games people make me play to get it.

The metaphor I use to articulate the games people play for money is revolution from hell. The players are these: a Safeway Sushi Chef; a Catholic Church Florist; and a Jewelers Servant. The Sushi Chef is a darkness you can see - you can walk into Safeway and watch her slowly quitting her job, getting drunk on prostitution in Las Vegas.

The Catholic Florist is proving sex is a fight when it's on camera.

Finally, the Jewelers Servant is defending her honor by starting the fire of concubines where there was suspicion of adultery.

I am so inside this metaphor that you can't hear me. The world hates you for knowing this much - count it as blessing and let's move on.

In the spirit of deafening noise I recall a character I created in anarchy and buried in anarchy, which is only conceivable in anarchy like being hated by the world.

The Big Guy was a mercenary and the unfortunate situation therein is how much financing revolution is financing terrorism.

River is the epitome of all this and the difference between myself and the dark lord is that I am safe and he supports her terrorism. Job, the cautionary tale from the Old Testament, is the horse that clarifies when revolution is death. The dark lord is trying to rescue a cheater so he is probably dead. I however, accept that there is an alternative where I reject cheaters for eternity.

The root issue is River's parents: I want to heal cheating, but the dark lord wants to cheat the origin of cheating. I am trying to explain, in literary terms, that I don't want to cheat - by giving Rivers parents a Golem-style exorcism and clarify that beyond doubt by contrasting that with how the dark lord is cheating her parents.

River's dad's object of obsession is River's mom, who fuels his megalomania, while the mother's obsession is alcohol. It is merciful to facilitate in them a sense of victory over their obsession. They must feel close to God in a way they had not before. River's mother found Jesus in a Panoramic Ocean Vista and River's father found Him inside while listening to Chamber Music.

This mercy is always there: it's C. S. Lewis.

––––––––––––––––

They were drunk on their death. They shot first, it backfired, and they are dealing with the consequences behind a veil. They did something very regrettable and that's why they are incapable of being honest.

Their intention was to play and someone died. They were forcing God to do something unholy and they don't accept that that behavior, immaturity, is unholy in the moment when they witness proof of how unholy their immaturity is.

We took the ice in a Viking world of reap-what-you-sow justice. They need a victory over their obsession with escape from death in Oblivion. Herod was thirsty for Oblivion and was immediately smote. Indeed, people in hell want ice, but Vikings are actually getting it.

This is not over, however, this is the point where the hidden sins become a nightmare. This bitch is too bad because it is close so I make the determination that there is no nightmare good enough to sustain the devil before you find pride in your division thereof.

The time has come when you should be the teacher but you need me to teach you. (Hebrews 5 : 12)

Verily, those who have worshipped the cross have crucified. The dark lord ministers to the dead and needs to focus on the living. He has bound himself to being dishonored in everything relating to the cross. That is fallen and "it is impossible for those who were once enlightened ... if they should fall away, to renew them again ... seeing they crucify, to themselves, the Son." (Hebrews 6 : 4 - 6)

Pilate washed his Roman hands while the dark lord participated from the Jew's side. It was full to help people, dealing in vacuums, but his pride in ministering to the dead is his fall.

The dark lord (amen) found fear in the cross and lost hope obsessing in that fear. His depression is funny to everyone else and that makes him lonely in any case.

The twistedness in the fallen is a willingness to help others spiritually but not physically.

The dark lord is asking me, "Give me one good reason why I shouldn't quit!"

He just needs to express his fear of the cross in a way that sells vacuums. He does not need to minister to the dead or the living, as he has been doing in the forest chapel.

Dogs are not out (lambs are not out) and this is the longest road to nowhere. This is withdrawal where you need to take a sign and cry. For River's parents it takes the death of their daughter for them to accept that they have a problem (first step.)

Let us cry a River:

Her father chose someone like himself for her. That is Adam and it made alcoholism very easy for her mother. Her father never things of being River's husband, of course, but her mother is always sad that way and it is an innocent suffering. She failed to change this sick, dance for Herod megalomania, but River was determined to change him. She failed as well. She was crippled to disgust her father. Her father was already dead. River's friends are drowning with her in Adam's covenant because a snake died and they still haven't registered that - they never heard the good news.

Who will pick up these pieces?

If it were up to me I would put their regrets on a desert island where they have nothing else to do. I would teach them religion while building a church. We would learn to put the faith we had in ourselves into the group. Finally, we would celebrate our victory over Adam's fall and christen New Eden.

We can't deny that River wants to marry her father, however. This hurts young men. When she was crippled she found another inappropriate relationship in the dark lord. After her accident she chose to hurt more men and my pleasure in her is to show how much she doesn't know that is death. Not only do I appreciate her ignorance, but more than that it is imperative to expose it.

Sinners are hiding and by buying this we are calling them out very bluntly. The only exception I make is to do it without using their names.

They are violent to themselves and blame others so there is no good reason to entertain their poison - they need to know we did not assault them and make the verdict stick by underscoring our innocence with the fact that we have not been assaulted.

RED

The Father is open to insult and praise but we can't expect peace while sinning; indeed, the promises refer to a Kingdom we choose or do not choose. There is waste there when we choose sin to any degree and that is spoiled. The gifts of God are complete unless we spoil them with such odd twists of circumstances.

The Son has a crown of authority to dispense grace and works of the Kingdom as well as the salvation to return. This glory is complete and it pleases the Father that he is successful. Our fear of unholiness is slain by His peace with changes in righteousness - His peace is magically independent.

The Holy Spirit of Immaculate Conception does glue the broken pieces back (together again, automatically) the world imitates the Father's Kingdom but the Holy Spirit breathes life into it. This is comforting hope that should be striven for to sow it in our future. The care of a loving mother would call you to it whether it is by permission or not.

We discover what a blessing it is to be prayed for when we are in the peace of the Holy Spirit.

Love, our heart's nature to act out virtue, is the law. "When Gentiles, who have not the law, do by nature the things contained in the law, these having not the law are a law unto themselves: which show the work of the law written in their hearts." Memory, like ink, recognized the heart [and forgetting our value (self-esteem and confidence) insults the Father.]

This sin (is opportunity) <u>to reclaim our heart</u> has a nostalgic, lavender roughness whose sweetness apologizes for any sadness, and the danger therein has its own <u>strange glory.</u> It is clear that angels grant protection in danger and having rest when you are attacked is brilliant love.

The rest we have in spite of evil has <u>a victory</u> (in it) <u>insofar as the rest lasts</u> - "I got mine." The wrath corrupting communication prevented the expression of the law. This goes so far as stealing wine from another; the victory of sharing a cup of wine exists in love and won't make you weak <u>when it is free</u>, to express its nature: when love is raw.

The invisible has a call or a smell and if you look at the sign you'll find the thing and make it visible. You can smell the marijuana but you can't find it - this from evil - which <u>proves evil doesn't know</u> they can find forgiveness and <u>victory. The illusion of evil is busy corrupting victory</u> (and there is a real need for validating success) <u>despite the real need for success.</u> Sin is bad - hide it in the garbage - <u>really:</u> pride is not throwing your sin away. Vanity won't throw anything away and pushes the furniture against the door like there is a zombie apocalypse, making fear.

"Would you like to buy a magazine?"

"I'll leave;" and then they'd be mad because they continue to sell their filth to an empty customer because they started and they can't stop, even when no one else is listening! That game is quitting your job. You need to know if your job is holy or play that game. No doubt, you want to save your job more than yourself because people depend on you. In your patience <u>you had doubts</u> only the title of holiness can repair - don't give up, <u>make it visible</u> and give your doubt to the cross. <u>It really is a call to a higher power - an authority who will bath you in their grace until you are full.</u> The cross is high in the concept of conditioning because it is unholy to repeat evil. I empathize with being the audience of fools - they were beating Jesus into submission all night before they killed him. It's a solidarity for tortured terrorists, victims of slavery, and unborn fetuses writhing <u>in the pain of a mother who can't hear them. Money gets its value from the civility of cooperation.</u> The wind either breaks you or you break it - you would live in purgatory if you practiced games with the wind. Optimism must break aliens and witches to condition success: Jesus was doing that work while hanging from nails. He is the king and he did save himself from an inequality of fruit - he destroyed all bigotry and prejudice by destroying his own destiny to deliver Israel from Rome. On one side of humility there are jews claiming omnipotence and <u>on</u> (the other side) is <u>a sober, free person.</u> Jane won't leave and she has no reason to stay - she found "humility" fighting the future with lust for every last man alive - real scoundrels too. (They found Medea's black lace.) Believe, habitually, that leaving is compassion for yourself: know why you're being sprinkled in gore and use that during your trip as validation of your freedom. (If you leave without a reason the devil will haunt you.)

You weren't killing the snake - you were in that circumstance. You were looking for some torture to glue up your gun or shovel. You told the snake it is dead but that didn't work. Gasp, I know, that's shit. Make sure the end is praying for them and the evil they came from. The evil they came from sounds <u>innocent at first, but</u> a little ink (mint) triggers the snakes <u>suicide.</u> Let suicide sacrifice evil: you are looking for love to fill empty spaces while the snake is taking what you put there, usually right after you put it there, and making it empty again. That futility belongs with suicide; get it back the same day - don't let the day end while the snake is bringing you futility. Replace the snake: Israel replaced their arbitrary shepherd-kings with a constitutional, democratic republic. You have to help yourself before you help others and the snake won't let you help yourself. Your best intentions to help others are destroyed by the snakes futility. Indeed, with a little effort you will survive the futility but, as much as the snake believes that helps them, I want you to find peace with their suicide like Judas: the poor need your help, not Judas.

Judas really believes love is broken and twisted in an essential way. Consider the facts, he kisses Jesus to show the thugs who to smash. Jesus couldn't be crucified unless there was the devil's agency of corruption present. Pilate <u>failed to judge Judas!</u> He had him right where he wanted him, guilty of insanity that goes far beyond medicine, and he let him get away. Why?! That negligence is criminal; he stopped piloting Rome just as Jesus was coming into Rome. His trial was supposed to be integral to His ascent and Pilate's jealousy of Jesus' grace betrayed Him just like Judas. They couldn't share with Jesus and that futility is a great key to success: throw futility into the garbage! There is a strange purgatory of snakes between futility and confidence <u>that sympathizes</u> with futility. Get confident right now - throw the porn away! The world is in the same crisis - it is a tool - if the world is evil it is because the devil controls it. <u>Trust is a matter of integrity that depends on all the parts working together.</u>

The law manages the illusions of sin to no end - you must break out of the illusion of sin or be bound in the law forever. That penitent stays "the penitent;" penance is the Rosary and the Novena goes down there every day in solidarity. It is a "valley of tears" full of "mourning and weeping" that cannot perceive any light: an inferno without fire: a black hole. You can witness the penitent but they do resent being watched - it's a bullfight - they're waiting for a chance to fight: there is a danger and it is a test of courage. <u>If you have any tendency for sin, inferno will desperately work to trigger that, for no apparent reason. Assuming you're free,</u> you will not miss - it was a small chance that you drink alcohol, smoke tobacco, or use real guns. (If you do, please die here because the rest of this assumes you are not a slave to ATF.) The hope of every creature is to be done and to have the freedom to exercise Christ: the American Eclipse.

The jew in high school is sexual harassment and hiding at home from the reality of <u>a world full of pagans</u> who can't stop crucifying themselves. Don't <u>hide from alcohol</u> - they'll find <u>a way to tempt the jew</u> in inappropriate behavior, like a slutty bonfire party that you know <u>dies in a DUI.</u> (Chris!) Before they get to A.A. do judge their <u>dog-like folly.</u> It's no fun to judge the penitent - get them while they're fools. You're forbidden from hating your brother except **when they're obviously hiding** a hospital-porn of sexual harassment - being creepy. They won't let you help and whine about apathy looking for excitement in all the wrong places. Why is my money no good? Atrocious <u>evil is doubt</u>ing my faith in the poor - won't accept that the VeriPhone works without prejudice and really wishes disgrace on American citizens like they're terrorists. Know there is a camera watching this jew hypocritically <u>earn a Darwin Award</u> while criticizing the most innocent. I hope you have something to add to that freak's show.

There is a ripe smell from rejecting the *truth* of their alcohol for <u>a better show</u> that has the best intentions for the jew but also recognizes the futility of their cowardice. You don't really want their enthusiasm - it's weak and they are in serious danger. (They need to be humiliated before they become a parent or accept more responsibility.) It's not really rebuking them - it's doubting their pride. Their show of pride is a popularity contest that denies no one likes them. They shut down higher brain functions for a coma of numbness where the king plays music. Their reward fell and they're wildly out of control being the failure they will later learn from. They don't know they're a god damned slave to the future and freedom is hateful to them thinking, "If I can't control the future …" followed by something really dumb. They can't find a hopeful future because it is innocent - the jew can't find innocence. I told them to eat shit and die because they have that destiny - they really must find the bottom, moaning and even screaming at God in a prodigal son's pig-pen before they realize they have lost everything and become the penitent.

While we are considering (the end of sin the terrorist, Hitler jew, is considering how twisted God is for allowing them to crucify Jesus. They don't believe Jesus resurrects. The kicker is that Moses is that mentally ill. We assume the patriarchs are all noble but they sacrificed their own to pursue a lambs folly - not so much out of courage but in a sick, genocidal justification) of Zion. They should have turned back when people started falling over dead, thanking God's providence when it was just mercy, not really destiny. Egypt gave them authority and instead of writing civilized law they fought the authority they were given. No one should read this and deny they have rejected authority - that would be very unholy. I'm thinking of an exceptionally rare case where the children of slaves insult the sacrifice their ancestors made to provide a better future by destroying it. When the victims cry to heaven that we are not strong enough to do this I want to be clear that it is not us but a tradition of Moses that persistently weakens people. I appreciate that cotton-picking slaves want to control the cotton without having that blood fade away into an apathetic oblivion of numbness.

Learning from failure is a reality and it must be done in planning - must not be a part of work. The night is ideal: set your clothes on the chair for the next day so you can wake up, take them to the bathroom, shower, shave, and dress. Darkness is poor planning: procrastination leads to pine; pine leads to cigarettes; cigarettes lead to alcohol; alcohol leads to drugs and that's all because plan A was procrastination, trying to find the cheese in work. Lent is a very private sacrifice that tests your plans and you learn from that failure. Procrastination is a violent spirit of antichrist that burns like inferno, inviting mountain lions to bite you. I found prayer in both cases, which lead me to headphones. My guess is that %85 of people do Lent and %15 do inferno. I take the odds to their conclusion and I believe sin is an illusion. I eat grapes of love: raisins, always going into mystery with confidence in humanity: I pass on crime though I can feel the violent spirit because it is hiding in a hell I can't find.

The devil keeps threatening dreams: sold the farm, exiled you, woke you up with apathy, stole your bedding, and tempted you to catch pneumonia like a lost lamb. I did it to show that choices are full of temptation and that the devil must fry for having any doubt: now I reckon doubt as the failure of choosing faith. The devil won't admit it failed to choose faith, is drowning in a purgatory of maybe. That spirit finds me all the time and won't choose success or failure, but I have this careful method of reducing not success into not faith.

"I haven't done anything wrong, I just sit here quietly."

"It's not enough, anymore, you have to choose faith."

Just sex, and you're either Dr. Ruth or you're Kevin. Backwards? No. Sacrifice? Nope. Someone is lying though. That hell is permanent: pride of vanity turns into shame because you can't have one without the other. Start by yourself and end up like Dr. Ruth. The link is bonding - sharing is controlling the growth of art. You can't start without a plan (I hate weak enthusiasm!) The smoke game was to start before the enemy with the cross - as a criminal - to pick a crime and then fight the enforcement of the cross, because you like to escape from the enemy. It's an illusion, though, because there is no escape from that hell and night falls. Escape never happened - your pine insults Joseph: it is too weird and long. The debt has been paid while slaves criticize the poor for wasting the cross. The cross is a necessity like water - we do use it, but it's not something to waste like smoke. That filth is obvious like zip-ties around your neck - a one way trip to death. Moses did that - they were were warned - and it's Coke: even Stephen: predestined - can't be fought. This fight has nothing to do with

<u>Christians.</u> There must be a way into hell without sin as Jesus does, like navigating a cave without getting stuck. Is it the first time? Or are you pushing a little deeper beyond the railing? Can you sense the illusion that someone else has been there? What ruin is this? Obviously the appeal establishes that the death of the testator is an illusion. Concern for the testator is causing a problem, but the jew likes the fiction and is sacrificing offerings to it. The appeal judges value of the illusion. Some illusions are transfiguration while others are hallucination. <u>Slaves</u> worship the devil of irritation like barking dogs and mosquitoes - they do it because they believe it has as much power over other people as it does over them. They won't change, but for yourself you need to validate that. Understand the alternative is punishment and the slave is a slave because they refuse to punish the devil, letting filth fester without flushing it with water. Affirm, with appeal, that you do flush.

Sickness and healing are Jesus' ministry and He gave His disciples the same spirit to sow the good news to all the ends of the earth. The appeal is His gospel - the words of life. The Pope spearheads the way of the Christian. Indeed, mercy has feeble beginnings in information but finds a surgical precision when that is performed. Sharpening love is cody - it's public. I am waiting for a sickness between the heart and mind to heal. Christ should be done - I should not have to correct myself. I was eating when the wind blew my hair into my food and I bit hair - pulling a bunch of cheese out with my hair. This is halo; I keep getting traffic that, while they come and go, corrupt my characters with ones that are similar but don't know the character's behavior is a formality - that I'm elaborating on souls Jesus predestined - <u>traffic keeps trying to change immortals into mortals - keeps trying to kill the good guys while I reserved that for River, the Big Guy, (and maybe the Dark Lord.)</u> The slave can't find hell? Then they pretend like it works. Then they destroy it. This happens to jews who lobotomize this message to cash in on whatever their shit is worth. They got the idea that what they want is hiding behind and illusion of danger and hustle like the trick is speed, but <u>the faster they go, the more gay (worthless) the shit becomes.</u> They can't slow down - can't get straight - humpty dumpty won't superglue like Frankenstein's monster - <u>there is no medicine for hustle.</u> (They have a little black book full of rape victims and when they burn it they don't get better.) The reality is no one wants to map that cave but that's the future anyways. (That orgiastic circus is where a lot of people became slaves to River - losing their minds and barking like dogs.) On the bright side, that hell goes down - packs it's bags and moves to Baton Rouge - so when they are remembered it's a lot quieter (everyone is afraid that hell is normal!) Really, everyone defends Caesar until that's ripe, and then mutiny. Everyone is afraid they are going to be betrayed. Futility is to God and then forgiveness, but you have to trade fear in for forgiveness. Do cash that shit in.

It is interesting to put the first toxic elimination in juxtaposition with birth: one is life and the other is, how do you say it? Dirt. Hard - really get up in this everyone has a single cross - "there is only one escape" and that is peace like water. Mortal Sin is bearing a sword in vain (like rape) in the back while you were blackout drunk! Leaks ash and would burn this - but also problems I can ignore. Venial sin is arbitrary, unclean iniquity unto iniquity, infirmity of flesh: oil and a short work on the earth like fish racing downstream (knowing the "wrong way" sign is their own work.) Blind and sticky foolishness from wasting wisdom: the dark side of money that defames itself as a Ripley's spectacle for the world.

Plan the intervention seriously considering the flesh and they found morphine but I asked for these ashes and I'll pass in powder until that becomes ash and then I'll appeal it with Hebrews because that inheritance is as flawed as the dead, even Egyptian Mummies, which is cheated and insecure, but (through the right cross) has been immaculately redeemed. Smoke the penitent: why mercy? Should evil be the punishment for disobedience? How can evil beget anything other than disobedience? Indeed (indeeed) master's touch has a softness that is equally forceful (in enforcing the insignificance of sin.) Be the change you want others to make: you hear this "give me morphine" and you hope it's holy! Indeed, there is no other side, which makes it recreational and you're like "that's too hard," right? That's this epiphany that the cross comes with morphine … "I'll never know how much that morphine costs Jesus."

Direction comes from a high place while holy grails come from a low place; if we are authentic we are actually leaving the physical change for the soul. Some people insist a cross is the purpose of the soul while I take a conservative approach in a "roundabout." You got it: the sin is the horse and those wings are characters: St. Francis brings a sick holiness. There is a lot of zoom in this "take off," like you were always high. The illusion of escape is the theory of uniformity: that we are many parts of the same body in the God of Israel, (but not in the corrupted flesh of the dead.) That leaves the flesh to a garbage dump and everything that is real is not destined for that hell. The storage bins in the garage are real, but both the food and the waste are hellspawn without the means to kill or even curse you.

You want, you faith, you get paid and in that sleep kill snakes (but that's down "there ...") It's all gifts in charity, but "want" and "hope" - want is futile - you want to like save money in a mutual fund and escape. So I'll remind you it was, at worst, morphine and what is escape from that? Holiness: escape from society with sinners by not sowing sin. Who gets paid immediately? No one - there is a temptation to credit yourself for work you will do and some people think that's business but it takes more need to make that as genius as business. Take it as a blessing that gifts are holier than darkness. Everything too bad happens at 3:00 AM - the darkest time; I do it - it's blackout! Let's find the kiss between that and dinner: closing the church, primetime, sunset, late, midnight, etc. kind of sunset ... right? (What is that veil??) Popde-cubes and Kenworth digital forum.

Flesh isn't the sin; the sin is cancer: healthy DNA gets corrupted by perforation when UV rains hyperactive particles of radiation - not cell death, but arbitrary damage - an ash that lives. Damage (that "off") is the sin and skill never looks at it. Juxtapose that with heroism and there is a fight for imagination. Charity is the Law behind Jesus' miracles of feeding thousands - bread is grass - it's only hard if you're unholy (then nothing works) but it's your own fault to miss something as ubiquitous as grass. (There is a beauty in the way God both needs grass and produces it.) The fear is being near an elephant when it loses control getting trampled in a stampede like Simba's dad. That was prudent to fear a God who smites with heart attacks! Who the hell is God?! This question is for anyone, like paying taxes - trick yourself with a new identity, find the gas, and let her rip! On one side of the earth people are doing that, as the sun sets.

As I go to sleep I kill mosquitos - I earn my "up" one at a time. It's hard to show heroicism like that - the meat has to be dead or a parasite - you can't drink alcohol in public. I do think saints start weak and grow their personal fight into a profession. The smell, then, is not futility; it was growth. Proof is always a family member intruding mercifully on a project half done: they take your oil and put some lemon in it then when you smoke the picture you're really smoking your brother's fruity citrus. That up fell and you became your own slave (but no one knows!) I'm trying to persuade people that's okay because someone will take that fight so you can keep going. The stopping is the game of tag: you tagged your brother and he'll tag someone else, etc. Yeah, I did not stop and my brother took my fight, but it's safe - I wouldn't share Mortal sin. So, that's the game: share nonsense: get your salt from someone weaker than you but also someone you trust.

Momma chicken has a lot of salt from her babies learning God - yeah, they got super stuck on this one! Yes, it is egg shells; they had "weird" shells and momma does that "weirdness." I think the father is hiding this innocence because they're impressionable and he doesn't want them to bond with men - that their father prefers women to do this like Little House on the Prairie. Teacher has a better idea - if you can, get it from them - use their rings. People are really sensitive about when direction dies in heart attack, really scrutinizing the value of every direction, when there should be priceless gifts (and not venial sins of budgeting.) **Contribution, when the sin is negligible and the reward is super-valuable.** That is the bow and it is so high it has special momma-chicken god-salt like, "that had a veil," and bugs whiz passed you while large birds cruise way up high.

Plan on being Jesus - it's normal for Him but it's kinda weird for her because she's very mortal while He is just waiting for you to die. You are sick to take the good with the bad - no one takes failure seriously - really concerned I'm watching suicide while I'm doing this. Should I wait? I waited - it's too late - I ignored it. Eclipse is (not a fight if you have) a plan and following it. They have all this plan from my work and they think it's soulful to die all over rocks that don't listen to disease. Loud enough that I can in my own better perception of soul make their suicide worse!

Validation like that makes them defend their soul while I was doing nothing against them and there, they have a crisis between crosses and roundabouts. Why don't they hide? Their end came and it's an awakening to hiding - they just met who passed on exposing them and now they know they're dead - it's their first time being dead.

Sending beauty to hell is much worse than sending ugliness to hell and she is so testing His halo arbitrarily: taking herself to insanity just to humiliate Him but it is the work you do that matters and there is no grace in her. This to prove grace is a failure at who grace comes abundantly to while the work is flourishing despite their descent into asceticism. (Buddha lost that fight.) Blood is her - she's got so many bells and whistles! I heard you're in sunsets like a canon as I obtained it; I would make that better with flags and trumpets, even the Knights of Columbus regalia. (They said it's the Coast Guard but she needs to work) on the grass. The blood ought to be cheese, juice, and grass - leaving the art to gastronomy. The whole is a body of saints like cheese, juice, and grass that is not just food - that is why it is real. The parts (fitly joined and compacted according to their effectual working) edify reality. This whole may have secrets that serve it but you can usually perceive the elements while they manifest! It was a clockwork grace (called "mint chronic") that only study (science in the empirical - objectivity) showed to a guilty audience.

Ignorance of heart is already hell - you can't break something broken. Killing snakes is symbolic but why the apple? It perishes nicely - like pine, there's a fight, but it's a *safeway*. The cool kids are programming the fight and the business is the fight. The dirt, the grass, the seeds, the irrigation, and the mutiny. Jesus; that's genetic engineering and horses; the horse is sick. Indeed, that's not here and it's work to get there. I am adding a liberal power to a design for a man with a throne and white beard to apprentice me and if it appeals to you I invite you to glow with us on like computers and televisions. You are high and it's important to talk about that. Fill some cups with tea, equal, sweet & low and then find the liquor in the cocoa-nut. Tate dog smells the garbage and finds an itch. There's a flash of insecurity because that's not how the devil does it - indeed, that up is very afflicted by chicken.

When I ask you, "How did you find futility in the garbage?" You start looking for forgiveness like you're in there. But you can't be that sick - it's not my problem. How do you tell the difference between problems to pass and appeal vs. problems to fix? There is a lid or a tie that seals it. Glue is too permanent. You're so shocked that this is a solution like it takes more rock or force, really selling fuel! You don't know where to put that - you're like, "If that's everything, I'll be in the garbage." You really wasted your dignity on escape and I didn't do that, so … I won't be responsible when this is misinterpreted as escape! Your original sin is a black dog I know very well: it's too sick to share the same bed! "I need space - it's your turn to buy toilet paper." So who has to move out? Who cares? The person leaving cares. If you really liked the bitch then don't get it and maybe she'll change - but if she was too loud then pray for them.

The shouting contest is domestic violence to them. They prefer Miller time to passive aggression. Yet, when you leave <u>the way you show you always cared</u> is very corrupted. Sounds weird, but we are keeping the end clean - it's a position of care we always expect other people to share. The other positions are all sin - the moment you stop caring the neighbors flag you down and that's because their leash only serves care. So we're in this <u>straight jacket</u> of care because the corruption is so deep in us we can't trust ourselves. Temple Grandin found down well like a professional and I'm faced with an audience who is still amateurs. They're telling me to wait for your experience … (is that blank pages?) Why did this application fail? If you won't burn this game I have to add something: consider Courtney taking Brian's checkout of cheese and vegetables. She is always there - don't mess with checkers. You do, but then consider Will's fight with all the ways he can design a website for a fireplace distributor - I know you care!

Senior Alpha's Easter Lilies want game and when you're full you'll pass out at 10:00 AM - waking up at night is exactly how far - then you're alone and Safeway is sawing denial of service because this is open but you're doing it wrong. Yes, it is perfect that game finds futility thinking that was the right way. It's not cuts - it is an armor of leather at immaturity. That game is mental illness, suicide scares, disability (can't hold a job) and they do get full - watching Stargate drinking Pabst until they have to move on to something constructive because they had an appetite for nostalgia (like the Odyssey) that isn't quite satisfied. They are amateurs because their art is fueled by mental illness. They are stuck in Original Sin like Jackson Polluck and their appetite for variety necessitates a fight for their mental health. Indeed, they won't be the prodigies that found the fight in third grade but it's not so bad - it just seems impossible in the morning. They didn't know nostalgia is futility and they didn't realize Odysseus got all his men killed by cyclops before coming home which is also futility. They signed up for the cross of Original Sin - which is cute like Adam - but only chicken seems to save them.

It's not sacred unless you are aware of this because this is the Holy Spirit of Hopi Humility (smells like a rosewood rosary) David's key. However, Original Sin is the punishment for digging in the trash. Basically the chicken was too sick to eat and you end up with a printer or something you don't need, which sucks because you really need a little chicken. There is a liberty to this law - you don't need to be sacred - you don't need this! You can camp outside the soup kitchen. I live in bread - like a piece of cardboard in the middle of a very large field of wild grass with mice, grasshoppers, butterflies, and birds. I know that's higher than cigarettes and I am saying that Valhalla is heaven while mental illness is hell. And this appreciates mental illness can't imagine heaven - I Philip James Renoud bring you God! Indeed, I'll have the wickedness that runs cigarettes as a footstool (more is!) I am keeping my spiritual armor in good condition for this work.

You're sitting on money and I'm not telling you you'll be able to buy what you want but you have to try - the only failure is not trying to find some clean chicken fingers. I know America trusts God the way they trust money - I know you trust God. We were not giving chicken gas - understand the gap between Safeway hot chicken and Safeway cold chicken! That's how far we have to go to be successful with our passion for coolness. You are not cool - you find reasons to reject chicken! Whine! Fear of IBS and sweat. I'm really not going into the Deli - it's not appropriate - and I'm not going to start any park-barbecue fires because I have alternatives (I'm in Black Forest Ham.) But when I put gas into your chicken don't reject it! We have to be cool to each other and let names like Nakita go and be what is in their nature - you can't bring alcohol to Nakita because she's too fast or make her smoke anything that's not in her nature to smoke. She is smokin' hot but we have to keep that cool.\

(The Island and) <u>Black Forest in the North is a present reality like the Hotel California</u> (but has improved so that it has clockwork grace.) <u>The church is spiritual</u> - like angels - <u>but</u> it <u>is</u> a world <u>without end</u>. If you're in then peace gets better for you - if not you have a growing appetite to test your strength and sweat for money. The Peninsula and Jungle in the South is a future of meat eaters who are artists of practicality that really need illusions to make sense out of the butcher. The butcher's election is the rose - everyone is smoking the first kill because they can't relate to an inexperienced butcher. The butcher has a final test that sends him North or he has an interesting life leading to execution. <u>Indeed, that is</u> (to show) <u>down</u> (to a blood thirsty people.) If he passes north it is to enter into rest much like death. The trial of peace is strictly southern while the progress of peace is strictly northern. This is the way it will be when Original Sin is fulfilled by the Law.

Eve had peace but she arbitrarily rejected it to be special - she had the element of surprise for a few hours and a curse of predictability for eternity. Her ignorance is cute when she is bound by consequence because she keeps running away to people who don't know but with law there is no place to escape. Consider "up codey:" found heart and the color yellow in, <u>oh, what?</u> The point of using the law like a recipe for love and artistic license refers to "service;" that North is raw God with a face that can pioneer an apocalypse for the South at any moment. Service is bonding and authority has a way of giving life to its creation (in great glory as it is written) towards the smell of eclipses. The weaving and tapestry are evidence of "higher intelligence" to a baser, primitive world of flesh. The Democrats in the South lobotomized their fathers in politics and they're the law enforcement. Reason is a rock: its value depends on how you use it. I'm saying democracy is not a rock and that its flaw is the "free market" <u>that does follow.</u>

The competition had a few losers who shouldn't have lost - sacrifice happened. That was everything but it was an illusion; they found combination wants three but it's more like zero! That church has a cross in unity because self leaves a trail of people (Jews) while *integrating* (Thesaurus.) The verb has an analog in the monuments. Fractals make weird monuments and straight to seeds that's before being filled up in the South. Their cycles of pistons power a change in the North's drone (Christ.) Yeah, your zero is a monument that mint(s) blood, in the United Kingdom. Christ's servant: Cody Smith, a worshipper of Josephs and the Virgins, Marias and Rubys (fresh.) They boy never killed even spiders - he took them outside with an honorable temperament. See how that should stay in the North because he'll get corrupted. Is the unity well with killing under *humane* conditions - is wanting sin having sin? The fuel is an illusion like clusters in honey because its matter is non-physical.

That bow is music with a skill for imitating manifestation - grow music and help a princess! Her friends had a sick event with her cousin around weddings (indeed foreshadowing) and everyone knows she is so destined to unify the already United Kingdom with *the Empire*. The outrage, then, when the garter turns into flowers! Original Sin and Charity is such an ugly smell I can't believe I'm so blind to the complexity (of garters.) Her friends thought she goes well with lust but I'm saying she is leaving her home planet for another where her destiny is stronger. That veil is two hundred million miles of clockwork and that system is having sprites. Only intelligence at the old planet from the perspective of leaving truly leaves. That eclipse is between suns in an hypnotic rhythm.

That sprite is other ships and packages. The older the ship, like a church, the better. Reliability makes me think of consumer reports but then there is faith in the model (sedan, hatchback, wagon, SUV, mini-van, pick-up, and transports.) Momma chicken's egg shells would be easier with a door. Some ships, like the midsize transports, can't exist without larger service ships. She is royal as well as harboring like a kangaroo (amps are warm.) She recognizes that fate is the world, that the Blacksmith needs repair. The robber got sniped. People should be careful about what they make (not what they destroy.) I heard they want more design and implementation ut I won't start over so all we have is exploring the faith of inter-solar-systems.

She hasn't explained that she has a regular, duty oriented relationship to her ship because it's so dramatic for the Man. She has some luxury that she wants and justice is either growing that (or taking it from someone who doesn't use it correctly.) When she tells him "down" it sounds like she is saying, "Get your own ship." He is in that mystery of being spiritual that is a judgement between miracles and prudence. (The first choice is a spiritual machine like the Old Testament incarnated Him and) the second choice is that Penelope has a son. Going with the son has baggage and Jesus wants her to go back to her father as well as the boys father so how did they get seperated and how burned is the world that is expecting her to give a damn about them? The boy has to be the prince of that planet and she has to come back.

When the farmer started producing more food than he needs he has a weird faith in like economics that makes him the key to a world locked down by Hitler. Indeed, surplus makes the illusion of Miller Time, like a cinnamon chronic from The Lawnmower Man. The line in the sand where I escape is between the graphic and the content: the tapestry has a snailey fractal map navigation which is way out of the features themselves. They said putting tapestry with farming was cold because tapestry is creative and farming is destructive. Orchards disagree: even if you're thinking the bugs and animals are fruit, it helps that the trees bear something besides leaves and flowers. I know, our reds are dramatically differen't like Naxis read a different Bible, and I am sure my Inbox Codey doesn't find exceptions, which means the cross is in my work.

To be clear, Christians do not have this fight with luck and I am using my high to talk down to them. They're like, "This guy is no better than you or me," but I don't get tired hearing it. At some point I'll get full and admit I have a relationship with Jesus that exists between apostles and really goad the jews for worshipping Moses. This saying disgrace is my passion takes some acquiring and it is good smoke - it's endearing to other saints - you would too if you could fight lust long enough to realize you're sharing death with people you really care about. Saving humility is to guide your wealth and I say it's trusting authority to both mitigate sin in the world and to amplify the consequence of sin in sinners. That's every fight, so, whatever luck is will be juxtaposed to liability limitation (disclaimers) and safety mechanisms.

"If I heal myself why would I hurt myself?" Jesus haunts. So, <u>we can start</u> to respond <u>by adding safety</u> to this thread. It's not garbage, I know he can get really sick flying where he has confidence like gravity doesn't exist. I need a physical explanation that uses gravity as the justification for take-off and landing like fuel consumption. He forgets the shit and that's not luck. More clear: woodworking requires constant destruction and design. They can't find confidence in a sure thing: they got stuck weird trying to keep it all while overlooking the big picture. Indeed, there is always a bigger picture. The criticism is palpable like Turing at A.I. It is proof that intention, or soul, is already here. They're intimidated by immortality but it's never that clean, it's never just the Hotel California, it's always intolerance to life more than eternal life.

Long leaks are paying extra for a warranty, escape mechanisms, permission slips, background checks, cameras, fog horns, and even water bottles. The quick leaks are safety mechanisms for crosses on the system, like the Blue Screen of Death veiling an "overflow." Titanic, the Iceberg; Challenger, the explosive scaffold; and, frankly, that's the jew, and so you're picking names. The Prince's life is the old glory of glowing candles: I was giving it to Penelope but she got full so now we're looking at children in space. I wasn't doing that for babies and concern (a wise prudence) for rape on ships (basically prison-rape.) Confident that it won't happen, I'm watching Him laugh at how ignorant we are while I'm sure <u>it's Halo.</u>

It's not too soon to punish nostalgia; I do it to emphasize my patience is a weapon. The song is drums in a Renaissance faire, medieval duel that mocks mortal sin. How far? Kisses, and that's them, so that's costumes, leather, robes, capers, and that's an illusion of money. What is spending imaginary money? Cash in your chips. We say Cody (is your life) because that's the Lord inside and we all care more about ourselves than about one's life it is fair. Get used to hearing that life is fair (despite that I'm going to repeat it.) You get a teacher or Behavioral Health Counselor; (that's regardless of sleeping with the enemy.) "I wish I was less like a vampire and more 'I have.'" Because your advocate is supposed to be automatic and you have to go through so much rigor to "cash in." There's the Constitution and then there is State Legislation and you're in a competition with California. Canada, and maybe Sweden challenge my authority to writing money but it's all one United Kingdom in Christ.

Fish don't want to bond like little rascals! Boo: felicity is a delicate creature fish are a *sick service* to. If it doesn't kill you, it's a worthless experience. Now, we have a flawed inheritance of a cross and Paul's slaves to shit and that must die to a new heaven like the north mega city. Snap and off … game over, the North has kept the south like slaves but they can't keep going down there. See Germany is the south, they're headed for civil war and Guadalcanal is how far. To that end, it's a communication game; Eve is a disorder in both animals and machines that has an alcoholic episode coming. I appreciate people can drag that out which is why I'm saying do it now.

See how bread is an audience elaboration on these themes of Jesus, which is the renewal of an old Jew hero, the Lord. When a prophet tells you who He is ou get a litany of names but when David tells you He is always winning a fight from a losing position. There is an old wall between quality and quantity but it's a lot like a turing test in that it is futile. I'm being Him for Him when He's ready to accept Judas is dead but He's looking for Judas while the wolves are picking off the flock in mass gunnings! Foreign relations is a system of judging the "others" that is fair but also has a shredder in the lower back. Before jumping to the conclusion that walls are garbage, see what's going on behind those walls!

They're *going on* like they're picking cloths and making a list, in codey, but they're not on. So I'm gonna say Judas is what they're forgetting and they can't be honest about what they're trying to forget. Judas is also forgetting Judas so it looks like everyone but me and Jesus are being lambs. "That's the accident," I intone about Judas. "I felt that," He affirms my sincerity about not repeating sin. But did those lambs feel any of that? No; they don't have to power to survive that Judas, or Eve, because they depend on that.

> "Should we stop that accident?"
> "Do you want to get published?"

He weaves this future into my presence. I know some of these moments, where Jesus is doing my job, are lost to me, and it disturbs me that He takes from me because sometimes he gives it to Judas. I'm thinking of the exchange rate of Philip for Judas and I owe Jesus a lot of appreciation for His dedication to hallucination - because I usually worship Him for transfiguring (renewing) my mind.

Let's say the way a computer processes information is the same as transfiguration. Children have to learn they're being treated like the enemy and get *smarter than the machine.* Rest is when your work lives and children don't know adults don't believe in their work. The book is passage, and the right, to rest. I want to clarify that "before my time" is beyond old; the line between sex and conception, which should be a precise art between two secure adults, is a tool from the future to teach children how to work with words. We're in a paradigm of systems that is cold and unmerciful to ignorance - the word Paul uses is concupiscent. If we're honest about how much there is behind us then we should be merciful to our ignorance.

With all the technology we don't understand in the Hospital specifically what value is there in study? I hear a lot of, "Just have a little faith," but that's my saw (and it's surreal to hear it from someone else.) I went back down to an old computer and those are still sick while the newest service pack is *coming down the pipe.* If you really study the old technology you're going to put on some absurd sin. So then what is (that nostalgia) repairing medical equipment? They took the cross, turned it into rapture, committed lobotomy, and that illusion is porn (like alcohol.) They really tried to hide the cross by renaming it four times (roughly.) Now they can't tell if they're on it! That luxury is the old computers and no one will ever take those problems seriously - no professional is qualified to repair systems older than XP.

Strawberry stripe was Safeway, the Food Bank, Calvary, and computers, at a law that universally heals the cross. Chris has that apple, soap, and rosary. That's altec lansing in the back (killing mosquitos.) Wow, what a relief, she was crying and I was doing nothing! (Best "Why not to smoke your mom.") Waiting this long is maybe sunblock but too bad so while the list of excuses is extremely long they are not, like ziplocs with rot, <u>the self defeat in not doing strawberry stripe is the biggest fire.</u> <u>Those problems are</u> just as absurd and <u>luxurient</u> (biggest fire!) that anyone can and should do. Watch Jesus' optimism as he goes on that cross and compare it to the sinners. Anyways, the end is the money: Jesus is rocking it with music while the sinners die in a shame of shitting their pants.

They have a scar on going on to soap - it is worse but words fail to describe the slaves arbitrary twisting against law. It's basically resentment they don't have - feeble attempts at blaming someone like Maria for not *saving him* with rape. That the end is vague and unsatisfying is too bad. It's not just one button, it's never going to be one button, it's always going to be a keyboard, you're all <u>drunk on mice</u> not considering code to be more than a single thing, <u>which is the library.</u> "Night and day praying exceedingly … in your faith." Paul's epistle to the Thessalonians reaches out … and His desire for this exact witch falls on pagans rather than the saints. I followed power - I healed women and the end is fruit. She was like, "Don't touch me there," and I did it first to show her the water down there is really tropical. The Industrial Revolution solidified the reality of "eating machines" that make their own fuel.

Moses can't control the power - like putting a forty watt bulb in a sixty watt socket, he dies early. That's the sin in lavender, that you need like two or three to do a single "application." You know how packages tell you how big they are? Yet one serving size doesn't fit all. It is too tight; it perishes and replacing it is the condition of this eternal thing. Germany wants to get *even* for WWII! They're bringing a storm; let's agree we want to know the details before we rebuke them. Which part of Germany is the plaintiff and which part is defending Nazis? The part defending Nazis needs to eat lavender. Bayer and other businesses (VW?) have complaints. Let's see, there was a depression and that hurt their economy. They took that very poorly - they did not *venture* far enough to reclaim what they had lost. So then those businesses that remained are complaining that they did not consume the remains of the dead businesses. I don't care for naxis but I also don't care for that negligence.

Before justice, there is a kind of money in the gains you can't see yet. Everyone's fighting over the poetry of that not. How should we speak of evil? River and the Big Guy are my kill list, what's yours? Don't say padlock Houdini - that doesn't work. Seriously think about your pit of darkness in your heart and how sick it is. There's lavender in white and that's soul - assume Chicken Soup (and Christmas) is going to reconcile the cancer in your heart. Then you'd be crazy to deny the pit of darkness is where your tears are! **Fushia** and *alcohol* are two things we're crazy to deny, and let's analyze why. Their patience is black like they're holding a water bottle but when there is no water they smoke. The sinner let sin run free and kept the love chained in their dungeon. Get even or smoke and that's not both; yes patience is black and white. Crazy is repression leaking and then it all comes out; someone is using control wrong: they were very carefully instructed to control the cross. Mint alcohol was like ninety-nine bananas, it was another *not* mixed with alcohol so you can love saying *alcohol is not.*

There is a bow like a lightsaber; one group favors remote controls and *lanyards* while the other is practicing Kendo. We're keeping it warm with waves, wind, a sea of glass, tire traffic, and white noise *nature sounds.* This up is sugar like birds and tapioca pudding. Pagans are covetous cross - that cross belongs to someone else. I suppose they're accounting for whose blood this is; the wrong is obviously dead but I didn't know them. Smoking problems are when you plan a fire and Eve gets hurt. Fog horns might be comforting like flares, but that's the car. They used to get distracted by me but that was self. I don't get noticed anymore because they know I'm doing self righteously. Self wrong got their attention but after a while the Father worked a change in their heart. They were possessed by my cross and came out confused. They are not my problem I use earplugs.

They have enmity for pagans (doing their job or living their lives for them.) I can see the penitent is on fire like a hellspawn vomitting on birdshit, and this is to change, but I'm not forgiving anyone who looks like they're about to hurt themselves. I think Brian is being sexually harassed! Pagans interfered with opening presents at Christmas and while they were doubting this found the fog horn. It means this is not their fight and they can't reconcile the old words with the new words. That's Bazooka Joe up (like) nacho bugles. **Sad christians don't appreciate their gifts**

because they did more than just heal or eat with pagans. I wrote, "perfection is lemon and chocolate," because I know that's the law and <u>it's eerily preminissiant</u> (considering some of use don't know what I wrote.) Someone trespassed and said the *no trespassing* sign is bad - the reality is a ban I need because angels are retarded enough to sympathize with courage.

The king has a fight: He is out but His *people* are not worthy of Him. They have orders from the world to sin and He has to convince them His life is better. <u>Fighting luxury naxis is an identity crisis because they kill (or worse) for the king's identity.</u> There is a much larger sin behind every sin - it's the treasure in the trash. That ends in the Biggest Fire, which is a political manifestation of River, the Big Guy, and maybe the Dark Lord. It is up, to say this is cheap. It haunts the horse to know they're helping the wrong people because they smoke that sinner with their blood - they alternate muscle groups and dance - they can really boggle a mind with bugs. That Original Sin shows up in forums.

Entertaining children has some weird stuff in it from evil, like hard machine stuff. You can tell which things are *backstage*, you know, and it's like the part that's for children is a cross. On one hand, the adults love to scrub and on the other the audience is not in. So, you're not in and you stumble at what comes naturally to Brian and me. Cab-Cadet is one of those things - when you fly a *cockpit* it looks really slave and difficult but that's the charm. You have to participate to appreciate the fruits. If you're still not in I'm warning you that the reward is not for you. Bakery is the same way - you have to help make the bread to gain the rewards promised to you. It's because the sin is willful - people criticize bread and that's a mortal sin. Accidents make self and criticism of God makes a devil. Those children are critical, like the twelve misplacing their sympathy on a crowd of people. (The risk was an illusion and they became the devil for prudence's sake.) Those children need to take their prudent criticism and put the bloody bricks back in the wall. Indeed, this is a tough crowd, this late in my career.

<u>The lamb can't find the courage to get professionally involved in their security</u>. Eve is putting this on really quick and it's the smell of growing - <u>that's for Ukiah</u>. People who don't like to judge consistently,

like: they can't find things in their face (can't hit broad sides of barns,) have a gay way of being black against care. That was debt at debt and the person who took the fight is no less suicidal than the blind sinner. That relief is no less suicidal than blindness and requires a system (codey) to find the problems and heal them; sinners are afraid that system is shame. Their debt is care: Strawberry stripe self healing and *mosquitos.* Indeed, I am justifying this work. Those fish are worst just before this, actually in church, when Andre's voice got dog-sick and he medicated it with a water-bottle. Those fish want to believe death is gain so bad! But I can't do this if death is gain and I am doing this!

Nurturing and dirt are the first division of strawberring stripe (*and this dog is pissing me off.*) The second division is eternity and circumstance. Suppose we just care, not really growing pumpkins, so then there's four. Expiration dates fell at the Food Bank in the name of charity - it's kind of *scrape off the mold* yet also *leftovers.* It's great, they are so efficient; their *sale* is extreme. I was explaining to Nakita that the garbage leaks and smells so you're in there already as well as being broken beyond repair. Nakita is hot enough to care about being broken beyond repair but Penelope has the computer to do it ...

Right down there with spelling and punctuation style is how much you can copy someone before it's sin. This defining General Knowledge is a witch hunt for the unintelligible words. The shredder is married to the unintelligible. *That's from evil,* and goes right back down. It was worse to give an expiration and use it, rather than find some value, but when do you stop being the lamb who wishes for ignorance rather than judgement? I have a thing with Odyceus ...

GREEN

Wake up or teleport? If you want this to be a dream let's nap at 10:00 AM. If you can really nap for like an hour and a half that's *there* very literally - your lucid dream is on! Otherwise you need to wake up to some lavender and fruit. That's washing: you can't win but you can earn a living. The brother's intervention is one of many interventions that can happen to you at any moment because we're *cody*. You said "this is cody" so often your *out* was to call cody *a lot of signs*. Bingo is a dog on old MacDonald's farm. A sea of glass is up from that farm - that's not here. Your mind is rocking computer like you understand what that light on the box near the power button means. That's shit so get the diamond: change is a substantial aspect of soul. As well, I'm confident justice is art so if the horse wants to be diamond we should value the contribution, even if the real horse is in a stinky trailer.

That shit's my shit because its maker's intention was good. If it's an accident of ir it's this kind of a <u>song</u> doesn't really matter - I'm not going to return any kind of confusion for earnest effort gone awry. Grape juice halo *had me at hello*. One sip and I died to that feeling: bread! I'm serious, I spend most of my money on it. It's not really bread, but it *goes well with* bread. That's her; so He's more direct. Babylon said that about wine or worse. I guess I'll do the logic on that one: "Wine (cross) *had me at hello.* I'm serious, I spent most of my money on it." See that's why ... I'm in dead center and the girl is the only other person here. This halo is empty in the middle!

I'm not really down, it's easy for me to expose jews and to expose their higher standard: what they'll get in recovery that's too *from evil* for them. Their *baby* is right here and wrong where they are. Why is no one doing Starbucks rape? You don't, but someone does: a blue-cheese jew gets too comfortable with alcohol and "I'm not that kind of a girl" is dead. So that's a hell where you're unforgiven. You're very forgiven when you cry out. The problem is *crying wolf,* obviously because we're (already) the wolves! If you want out it's this far! *Getting it*, like ring rang, is cody (like buggy) and a real even, but will is the spirit. Their strawberry stripe is broken on alcohol and they put whiskey in their soap. Yeah, they die right there, trying to get up from *one*. If God was that sick He would not exist in any way, but He does, in power, and the power (which jews are not) has life.

Rube Goldberg has a fight to keep *the momentum* going with fuel. Candles burn ropes that drop weight and drive a fan that pushes a teetering ball down a track to no end. That faith is low like protecting your shit, it says something about dignity: the symbol is a ball and the illusion is the fuel but the fuel is dead and I'm saying dignity suffers when the horse is the world. It's the same thing with candles in church: your prayer candle dies after *a while* and that's not ink like this. I was clear that is the fate of some of these books, but that fight is good because it's like five percent and I like a hell that lonely. I'll cut that hell so easily and bless them because it took one little sign for me to peg them as dead. I'll be asleep and find them like a mosquito. I wonder what attracts them, but I would be careful to not go beyond and kill my little friends. They're saying I can't bait mosquitos.

Dignity takes a beating when you break six: it is a reputation (or merit) that is other people's faith in you and it's weird - it has to do with integrity. I don't mean it's chronic, I mean it's *maintenance*. I said the cross hurts Jesus' dignity like a prophet in their own city. He survived - something survived - but he did lose dignity. Yeah, over the next couple thousand years he got it back. Harm, yes; care, no. He goes, "it has been reconciled," but that's shit because people still suffer persecution. Indeed, you can feel how grievous Senior Alpha's cross is when you care about dignity and I know people are guilty of diving off the cliff of their own dignity. "You don't know how it feels," they say … but Lent is that! Know we don't talk about dignity (right here.) In the future we will, when it's free, but I keep insulting people who deny their dignity has value and that has an end where they accept I hurt them. They can't accept vulnerability to the cross like it's mental illness but it only takes a few minutes (up to four hundred years) for them to utterly perish. I've seen it enough to know their denial of the cross is real.

I saw a new image on a karaoke bar of a football player charging through snow and I think that captures the smell of luxury (naxis.) That inner man is a cross: a grumpy grump (crabby.) They can't show my inner man - their best is Loki's coptic rose: our Lady of Guadalupe, but that's humility (I'm not that feminine.) The details (description) of my inner man are Chris in the morning, Daily Church Service, this Conchita logistical fruit, the King James Bible, and then a polish cheerleader. It is evidence I am holy and pure: I hide nothing. That up is tennis, marriage, and volunteering at the food bank. I became the subject of my study of Jesus. Recall that Jesus is way higher than Paul, or even Peter (as well as Mark.) Paul is a pattern for the worst because the jews are not worthy of Jesus' patterns. That's the hope of rest. The priest has a giant red book he keeps in the sacristy and that alone is a good reason to come to church. I am saying rest is in the church, not any private study!

There's two ways to do *person*: a computer and an asian start near the beginning but eerily far from the start. Do it or let it happen? I *do it* very little and if I do it's very - very slow: five minutes per sentence. I chose this from a long list of options and it is temporary but we know it is the experience (the journey) not the shredder at the end. Hot? Cold? Sick? Those are relevant to every person much more than their merit. That's why this leaves Penelope, because she's a trophy! They're saying I can't do that - I can't make my laurels - but why not? Yeah, so good luck, right? No, actually I have a few tricks up my sleeve. They would do person my way. Now, we have the mind of Christ, not the mind of the world, and, indeed, it is cheating to the world. I really don't care for who is in front of me. Yeah, this was Paul Bunyan, I am getting luck from living out of a backpack like watching God *Galaxy Note* my prayer in *shooting stars* while I go to sleep. Luxury is sin: be the horse or die of regret!

Straight up is my fight with Library staff and I don't think it's just this library. You can see they're not helping any homeless people get published. That's negligible in that they're hiding computers - that's why this title is Codey - I know computers so well it's a sin to pretend I can't reproduce Codey with books (instead of a computer) but they're saying computers are the only way to get published. Geist are my secret; I walk circles and watch how they change - that's geist. Tree formations, signs, numbers, flowers, birds that hang out on one side of a fence and never on the other side ... weird stuff, but stuff that has bearing on the future. Baby? *Only one I got.* The computer analogy of this is trends - you can make luck by following how really high websites change. I was telling Jimmy that I'd set the world on fire by making a program that makes money and all you'd have to do is run it ... but that's investing in Google ... now you're in.

You know I invested my soul rather than money I can't be sure I deserve. Why high? Efficiency and grace bear fruit; that is time: put good in and get better out. That is up - higher up! Yes, right now. There is a strange temptation to assume old evils have been saved. My ugly is good but that's higher up; no? I heard the good songs on the radio and when I bought the CD I didn't like the rest. Free is still better than the purchased possessions and those are even greater than debt. (Get that dirt - anything - is better than debt.)

The merits are coming from different directions; one guy is classically trained and smoke the Bible, and the other guy is a college teacher. The *arrangement* is like a geist, you pray for good weather and the right conditions but God is always a trend you imagine you are curling with fine adjustments towards His goal to award experience (before it can't continue.) The dignity! The person is responsible to use their life: food, work, and leisure, to influence their person along their character to align with these universal geist and in that victory earn dignity.

Cody and Nakita are still living with Nakita's parents: the wood is glorious light and those lambs love tea. Boiling water is classic and Cody does all the sickest jobs because they're easy for Him. Not a problem for the baby - it's just words - He doesn't have the weakness for temptation all the other lambs suffer from. Babies are good with temptation and cutting through red tape. It was only after temptation becomes a sin - but Cody and the baby never fell into that vicious circle. Indeed, the law is prevention and it <u>only becomes punishment</u> (when its purpose dies to the cold reason of justice) <u>when there is no alternative.</u> The impressive part is that he left His family, a mother, Jacob Smith, his brother Apollos and sister Madeline, as well as the farm, without sinning. Those birds are very well - surprisingly well. I'm saying you can't find this hell of butchers and blood that is selling corpses at a very high price because there is so much demand but when I tell you you're escaping the Titanic like an aristocrat your guilt is palpable so we'll have to look at why you can't take a gift: if you're reading this you should enjoy watching justice ... really love justice!

Someone realized the cannabis is on the sinking ship and they're like, "let's go back." So, then the crack is not for people who just got out but for people who have been out for a while and how they're using it to *solve puzzles.* Those people, those puzzles, and their minty-chronic that shouts, "Everyone do it like this!" (Oh, that no one can hear them!) I'm talking about children who dug for a way out and got really dirty with no success: every dog. I have to remind them the baby is crying and they're the baby because they keep *maturing* the wrong way. The corrupted children are in A.T.F. while the wolves are in the marijuana. First thing: it's legal and it is persecuted. Second thing: the corruption is shit. See that there is no lambs (corrupted children) in the future because they all turned into wolves that laugh at how they used to fear a clean mind. Everyone is waiting to say those lambs are shit but they're gonna have a fight with prophets telling them they're <u>not out from beyond the grave.</u>

Yeah, there is no beginning

My mother is medicating victims of my father who died from the exotic nature of the void from before creation. Their names are Robert and Catherine Cooper; their condition requires fortune, wisdom, and hope, but doubt is the problem. They have an obelisk from my father, but the message is insane, it reads, "Writing on the obelisk," in a mysterious self-reference.

So, the observation reveals a tendency to start over and once that happens a second time the new beginning is observed to correlate with time. Knowing this much was temptation for Eve, but the Coopers are different - they do not repeat history - they anticipate Eve at every event, tag her with a scarlet letter, and expose her to their friends.

We're going to do that with escape - we'll do it once and then when it starts to repeat we'll observe Eve in it. As great minds have suggested, escape comes from working together: when civil war erupts in Africa, the U.N. quarantines them. A second event is alcohol poisoning in Ukiah, California: a vomit covered sidewalk in a dark desert of pine and unrequited love. We can't all work together while the anti-christ is preying in Alcoholics Anonymous. The Dark Lord is probing the mystery by betraying himself. It's not over until he makes himself cry. He isn't violent - he is trying to stop violence - but he isn't helping; it's all to the dead from a safe distance and the Dark Lord is too safe.

Babies cried because undoing the hate requires a leap of faith from the Dark Lord and he won't do it. All he has to do is change but he doesn't want to be forgiven for making babies cry. With a little effort, so small the Dark Lord doesn't even notice, we surgically removed the cancer that pressured him into betraying himself. As expected, Eve is the cancer.

It's alive! (It's my mother.)

The same thing took place on the Delta and the Big Guy had a heart attack in that anarchy. My sympathy rejects declaring them since they are no longer oppressed and it is very dark to recall that since they have been forgiven. Everyone is helping me do this so the emphasis is on how honest this work is.

We concluded that the world needs more mid-size transports.

The work has been organized from large to small, beginning with a macro level of Cabin-Wagon, and Trailer. This level is framework the crew sets up with robots. The next level is automatic and is also preparation, using the design the Fixer made to turn it into a set of instructions. The third level takes the instructions and materials from the initial state to their final state with events. The events are said to conform to a fractal reality that is negligibly close to reality. Finally, the fourth level is the material itself, which is my mother; (clement, loving and sweet Mary.)

Nakita is a mother but she is not my mother and her mother is also not my mother. These mothers are being the baby but we had to grow up to have children. Long story short, Nakita is putting her mother's immaturity before my mother. Opposite to the way that Jesus is Lord by serving others, Nakita is obsessed with hierarchy. I mean she is stuck being a middle-man between the Lord and developing nations, even after leaving the delta, because she Lords where Jesus is humble. So she is learning to pray rather than use money. She is cooking less and exploring nature more.

Cody doesn't understand a lot of what she does because when he gets close she changes. She is learning that honesty is sweet and secrets are bitter. Finally, she is accepting that her reflection is hard because it is some back-woods, inbred disgrace that people laugh at. She is beautiful, but mirrors are bad with identity like time-capsules: they lie (you don't really know what is in there since it was made.)

She has itches only hard things can satisfy, and it has been a matter of my prerogative to give the nasty ones to River and the benign ones to Nakita.

The fire has been claiming Cody, but that's immature. Nakita is medicating the devil and people give that a veil, but it's my work to show that medication misses a spiritual sickness - that it is unfortunate and the real issue is understanding fate as a subject of holiness.

"Everyday is a winding road; you get a little bit wiser." (Sheryl Crow)

So the elderly are really high! That brings up the point that Jesus is the oldest - that He is the winding road.

This is funny: Cody and Nakita have the same lack of experience in dating as Jesus. As well, that seems to be the problem. When it comes to the home and the home's place in the world, they appear to be ignorant. There is simply a list of things, concepts and skills, that they need to either Google, research, get trained for, or start from scratch. The *baby* is home-improvement.

Law enforcement has done this. They have a Bear Patrol out in the county there. The Law stops the anxiety of trespass because that takes confidence in the lives of the people that enforce it without mistaking their relationship for anything other than "power, Holy-Ghost, and much assurance." (Thessalonians 1:5)

Cody needs to focus on the baby by teaching her how to read God. He says, "Look at the birds, they're talking to you."

"To you!" they reply.

He talks about God inside and out, forever, amen.

All this genetic engineering and artificial intelligence is in a sick disposition. God never did that: we find life goes back before the miracle of cell formation, even suggesting we will find aliens to be very similar. The laws of nature reveal an energetic rhythm that exists *outside* of space and time. So what's the ghost and what's the shell? Angels are the ghost but the shell is so big we're looking at an Aion, Secret World, Shadowlands darkside that allows us to control computers. I keep that *bridge* but I'm in bread now. So I was not getting rewarded, FunCom never sponsored me, but I'm taking my own rewards by nurturing Odyceus with bread. Yeah, I'm buying paper for that. That's the mint for being *genuine*. That different without sunglasses and bags, if not your whole *outfit*, should be Christ.

Stop searching for that and take up a search we started. Turn it into a book and return the revelation to us. This is my work in the search for *Codey*. Prototypes test the theory, giving you *ballpark* information about the subject. Two main categories of Codey are abbreviations and matching. One is naught and the other is comparison (or contrasting.) That naught can be; that's making money and it does leave a trail of prototypes to achieve that. Credit is the achievement of developing prototypes *into their eternal form*. That spirit is, "Keeping the faith," and "staying the course." Here's the hard part: that's keyed up like a soldier who can't rest. The world is what happens when you rest before you finish searching for the rainbow at the end. That doesn't work, they lose things and never get them back. They were searching for death, the limit of what they could lose. Search for something real and holy to build yourself up - indeed, credit yourself.

Delila's poetry is a machine: staff screens calls, relays a list of stories, she picks one and goes, "I'm sure we can find the right song for you (and Shirley Temple.)" Haunting chords and the other people are like, "I'm in that." Will hit those people like Thor: cracking *back* lavender. It's healing and may cry suicide. Ritalin took a ride up to heaven and lost it over a vague horizon of molech like robot wives. This is codey, you think you need all this but you don't. You aren't like me and I'm close to comparing you to parasites again. No, I said that's shit and that salt is melatonin: your sleep schedule and mine are clashing. I said most people lie in wickedness and "I'll kill you in your sleep," and it works! The poetry is it is mercy - it only happens to people who are *way off the map*. Fringe? Prevention? *I fought authority and authority always wins.*

This is nonlinear like referencing: just find what you need and keep calm. Adding to this work changes what I did but also what I did not do. I'm going to *cook* that not until it's <u>ready to be filled</u> (produced). I heard writer's block is a failure to move passed a particular subject - a failure to accept work that is nonlinear. How's it gonna be? Exactly like this: a cathedral of Holy Spirit, forever, unceasingly bowing down to a crucified Jesus. If you don't like it now you're unlikely to change. There's a house, garage, and publisher that don't exist yet but drive this boat and you have to decide if you're on this boat. I keep talking like I'm in the forest for the sake of that coke. Eventually that coke expires, in *rain*, when this goes *on* for a lack of willingness to *tog* in here. That's the boat, like Noah. That is down (the father) and refers to bedroom offices. Now, if you see this *office* as a cross, then down is up. (Indeed, this is more of a cross than an office to say writing is a bloody art.) I'm saddened by the competition's lust for this blood when they could benefit in heaven more by seeing the cross rather than being on it.

The shit is bait and I didn't choose it - Rome and the United Kingdom took these shots from very far away and I can't change that fast enough. America is taking its manifest destiny back but the process has a lot of *putting on the cross* that puts the cross before Jesus in Molech Luxury Numbness. If you stay low, like a Ninja or a troll, then you'll find the cross in shit in such a way that you can't avoid it unless you find a better soul. That's glockenspiels at turbos and the Antikythera Mechanism at computers, but still torture for who made it (the only alternative is to pioneer the future in the present) because <u>waiting</u> for it <u>is torture.</u> The justification for the cross is sacrificing the future and it is a sure hell when you replace Him with her. You're the pie and if you can't help yourself it's not my fault. If you have to use your coke it makes no difference to me (like that, do fall.)

University is Michael, the only way in is admissions. You can't accidentally hurt God: you can't reject authority and play God. Delusions of grandeur stem from universality but when you give that up in mock-humility you should know that's not really in God (and never was.) You just have to do it someone else's way until you can share that way. Bad up is up from evil and I don't blame anyone for how much this work is bad up form the Big Guy and River (except themselves.) So, that company is guilty and it kills them softly to expose their rejection of authority and *even* their peers. The circumstance is the problem and I'll give you a few examples. River has a Bible but she can't use it because she is unworthy. Saving the Bible is removing the River from it: see that fight is so fire! Difficult customers corrupt the library and you have to smoke marijuana in the back to get that game out. That's why I asked the staff to call the police. You heard me say Jesus has a cross in unfortunate circumstances and you need to adopt that starving child.

I struck a chord of denial on ¢50 / day. See that Michael is no less than writing a budget. Actually look at whether your budget can give something back and use the charity to improve your budget. I don't care how good you are - I care how bad you are and what I get to do to you - you had rights until you became a criminal and those have no excuse. Those open wounds cry and I can't do nothing. That dirt is cripping and heart attack: I will be that wolf. God doesn't heal dirt sometimes: specifically when it is %100 dirt. Pure filth gets an expiration date and a veil: I don't negotiate with terrorists. The circumstance is dirt and, just like when you die (a holy death) that dirt goes *down* into a grave while your spirit is free. Egypt is harboring some dirty mummies because it won't let tomb raiders trash their dirt. You have to be better and seperate the eternal parts from the temporary parts. They're taking nonlinear games very extremely poorly in sweat, blood, and tears. Play the computer and lose but people suck at nonlinear games so get that chess (as opposed to a game of life that goes education, career, children, luxury.) A local *vaporium* had a universal chess game in their window that said, "It's your move." Indeed, that sucked because no one would come in claiming to be god and play the game. (That opponent was artificial.) So Brian and the Man are essential for games but it is more valuable if I am the Man and one of the readers is Brian. Trolls rage quit and read a book but now they're rage quitting this book and it's a sign of the times: everyone is retreating from others for a closet hell they think is better. It's not better - the machines are unceasing and never sleep - I hate explaining the omnipotence of machines to megalomaniacs (who think serving machines is better than donating ¢50 / day to starving children.) Boo. Shame!

So, I watched someone die over a two year period as they tried to possess (the future) with witchcraft but I told them their magic was weak! That seems to have pushed them towards *using* their death (to possess it.) So now they're dead and some foreign businesses are replacing him with the actual factories he couldn't create. Start by yourself and drown in lust or wait for others and do it as a warm community. So, wrath aside, my opponent, Brian, really likes other people. The same jews that are creepy stalkers think pain is out of being stalked themselves. River is punishing herself for not getting raped while the Big Guy is doing the same thing. The weird part about the Big Guy is his rejection never happens because he's so punished there is no chance he'll ever confuse his suicide with River's. While River and the Big Guy dance like that they forget justice involves other people: watch how Brian is jail bait for wannabe Penelope's: he shreds fake dignity with real dignity.

Is the hospital just for pagans? No, those are long leaks, you're supposed to have checkups and keep a close relationship to a doctor like He is Jesus or Joseph. I don't care about your relationship to your doctor because I'll never know: I am on the out-patient side and whether he hurt or helped looks all the same to me. Law doesn't have that freedom, and again, I will consider every fringe idea the world can come up with but retain my freedom; I'm not concerned with how predestined those hells are. You do six or you don't but if you do you can call it whatever you want to; I'm still giving you the christian equivalents because there is no excuse to fail to find Jesus in these supernatural forces.

If you're a lamb you let your person happen: whatever college sends you an invitation is the college you'll go to. If you're a wolf you'll make the choice to go down into a library and prove the spirit is alive by the renewal of your mind. Merit is for lambs who are limited (indeed, higher) and paper-weights to wolves. When I say I'm making myself to people who are incarnations of Man (Adam) they protest that we didn't vote and the process is corrupt. I have to keep reminding them I chose the last merits: what Adam left for dead. I'm very careful and it pays to be slower than Adam; I profit from exhausting the world. The weird part is that I am slower with words inside the church; I'm using all of *it* at about five minutes per sentence; to use the signs outside coherently I have to turn on metaphorical gas - those signs flash instantaneously - signs in the outside world (city) are absurdly quick and emphasize Jesus' resurrection, dipping (too low) like the cross is easy?!

Changing light bulbs is a service and there's a sick way to help but it should be straightforward. I know it seems like *turbulation* (waves) are why, but not so much. If you follow me, I'm saying transfiguration, the thing that happens when you exhaust CPU's, is light, but then why all those pixels? The light next to the power button is very different than the monitor pixels. No shit? What if the maker fell? Then you need a stricter law, but where in the law? Your wish is that experience of this light is forever - is priceless. Yet it's not perfect and cats are placing bets on why. When Jesus fails he makes light: indeed, I did say that service is sick because they were not successful. Their intention was good, and they only made a venial sin, but their accident is bad. What do you make of this mild human error? Cartoons - because goofy doesn't care about excellence. You can't save them? You can, but honestly cats don't let you change, and I've been so persecuted for being one of those cats.

Jesus can kill, reserve a separate *reality* for sin, and have bad accidents. Those are Revelation, Harvest, puzzles, *down*, pressure on open wounds, triage, and healing soldiers. That's enough to end a game or two and I insist that sick shit comes out. I'm not just selling dreams: I have to prepare the future for these dreams or they won't happen. The poetry is right on the line between impatient and necessary; I was saying, "I'm gonna have to start something." The *fluid* is so smooth it looks like a mirror; those skipping rocks are light like panning for gold: the world is coming in here! What makes manifest is light regardless of purpose and that's why all flesh comes to Jesus. That life is hard to sell with a cross in it, though.

The *penrose* is a holy bonding experience where you cross something little, like a pen or a watch, to throw down some sickness where Cody may have exhausted the *specialness*. I can't know how special I am and I don't take it personally when Bic or Civilian are code blue. Little blue insists hard is little and I get harder so pulling back the curtain is not for the little ones. I can't see them but it's still *abra abra* … Why? They want to change the law (Christ.) Operation of God is from experience and distilled into memorable phrases. That is folk and very sacred; it is a gift that rewards correct behavior. Cameras captured it and then coach modulated the film, putting *empty spaces* between frames, and careful study emphasizes some aspects while garbaging others. That study is Jesus and the nostalgia is garbage. Open up the dialogue: beginners use a little legal pad on a clipboard with a church pencil. Experts use notebooks and pens. Seek up: that's the horse! All of the way to a four hundred year tradition of America's flag.

Hollywood is full of hypocrites who lie for money because they invented too many evils. The other side is service but people aren't dividing love into illusions and service. Illusions have to make you sick to believe them and it's called gains, but there is a difference between net gains (real) and gross gains (illusion.) Service is wasting their energy on illusions while deer are laughing because God provides for need but services are drowning in their clients sickness like a lifeguard without a floatation device. Deer glory is seriously mocking luxury.

When you have children it is supposed to turn you into a cody wolf with a sensitivity to your baby that forces you to find a sensitivity to yourself. If someone else did your cooking, cleaning and entertainment I hope they won't for your baby to teach you the tough love (for your dignity and for your life's sake.) Your *tight* will be that wolf and River won't so she'll be in A.A. or have her baby repossessed. I'm watching what A.A. does to witchs thinking they finished before learning the steps and I know their pride is balking in protest. You're this explaining magic to gentiles: first it's the baby - then it's a pregnant baby - then it's a car. It's either a family tree that doesn't end or death and I am saying fuck you to anyone who isn't having children (sorry priests #DeaconOut.)

Leaving Penelope is very popular like Ody - assuming she has a future that is incorrect - this ginger has no future because there is no other lavender. Ginger is trying to marry lavender but that is not. Here's *broken beyond repair*: a slow smoke of fat southern bitches where you can't tell the difference between eating food and being eaten. Blessing has a darkside insofar as faith has a curse; the fractal you're crying for shows a pattern of curses, twists, and justice. That break is smoke: a tiny crack in faith that is like an old man making luxury out of death. Game over, I'm healing those cracks! You have heart attacks scheduled and the intention is too bad. Your greatest strength, insofar as it has cracks, is your greatest weakness. That game was heaven and earth and the end is a world that has accepted Jesus' gift of eternal life.

Thanksgiving has so much plan B; the greater good keeps moving around and, like Atlantis, it is never in the same place twice so if you leave the greater good you'll need a miracle to find it again. I can't emphasize that enough and it turns into a lot of nods and affirmations. I don't understand people who take our collective gifts personally. That down was too high: it was real but not at all intelligible. That was like meat out the airlock.

"Anymore?"
"I didn't agree with you!" and it is fine.

They were talking to God and that doesn't disturb my piety at all. This late is from evil because I did wait and old men are doing it. I am the edge of the knife - I am modern and authority. I have the hive's power and it is like ten times harder than doing it alone. That's this Yankees moneyball where the sugar and spice wins. Self was an accident and I laugh that my accidents are the best.

I am the Lord [(this is law) but who is the apostle?] of Christ as *the faithful* spirit of peace and prosperity! Gaelic whispers in your boat in mp3 as wild clouds break overhead. She said, "Grace; be to you …" in my head (for me,) in haunting poetry. It is rare that you see all the parts change at the same time, that's the inversion. They can't determine if Christmas is the top and their luxury is cerebral. In Christ we put the eclipse first as *the faithful* with "lowliness, meakness, and patience forbearing one another in love; endeavoring to keep the unity in the Spirit (of the bond of peace.) *That ye might be filled with the fullness of God.*

Cinderella is my humility and it's a great place to start. Is it in bad taste to suggest her sisters can still betray her growth? Criminals interfere with investigation so no: foul play is four. Most of the physical universe is dirt (wow secrets?!) Something about burning water … that *on.* Good, let us talk about library computers; trends are the seeds you pipe into Inbox Codey. Baby powder poetry: lavender, drones, Deacon Keith Fournier, artificial intelligence, etc. That mystery has a fight with Ody; the pagans use Odyssey mercy to justify this game of Cinderella … and I haven't complained about this assuming the cross is just: its coke and an egg shell to grow out of. That's hard to break out of so that up is a little broken, yet do fall and make a note of each thought. That bread is studying works. Yeah, reason fell, so that indeed is fire. The value is arbitrary - say it is expensive - but motivation is money and you need confidence that will work.

Assuming this is tears, you're looking for *meaning.* They said that's ice-cold glasses of milk or even ice-cream. I have to warn you you are biased and direct your attention to the cross. I usually don't do this, but let's say the cross is unintelligibility, the opposite of meaning. I have to like Disney has to kill Bambi's father. Is it my fault? Really? How can you make that right?! I want to appeal to the Queen! "Your kingdom is in shambles!" Who is the authority because I might be more intelligent than them! At even, I might move to the capito instead of this *band-aid* treatment. How much would it cost? Ear muffs and ear plugs, a bicycle, and bust fare to a more civilized world where money buys happiness no matter how rich or poor you are. "Your money's no good here." Heartbreak in all the right places and skyscrapers where there was a hike. That *glimmer* …

Judas is romancing and not: the romance is a service (he secretly hates them.) <u>That is a secret,</u> but what the CIA does for republicans is no secret: their shit is clean. Do fall into denial. Does it make wrath? Yes, but I didn't do it to you. I just said Judas makes wrath and no one saved him but Jesus was saved and this is from evil. People have so many names for the devil it is a mystery. There is red tape, but Jesus won't use it for shit and I'm investigating the criticism of a book those sinners refuse to read. Stay thirsty! I did lambs exhausting welfare vs. the Bear Patrol (Game Warden.) When a real witch comes along you can either study them or the black plastic bags (*rape mattresses*) no one comes back for. Indeed, biographies are too many (too long) to study and you need witches like St. Francis to integrate the information. People are spending their lives on Ody's suicide instead of hugging Jesus. One part of your royal treat men has to be the best and that is Jesus (if not St. Francis.) Little children, keep yourselves from idol mercy <u>that will not survive crossing the street.</u>

I think pets are dead already and that it's unwise to sleep with those pagans. Black and very common, like rape in the world. So what do you do if you haven't met your spouse but you're sure you want a family? Your father knows? Now - you know He's the parking attendant. Where? The *Man's father* likes grace and He has it: he isn't driving anymore but he has a list of things he wants from His father and it's good to be Santa. Here's the awkward fact that charity is better than you think it is. What is saving grace? It's prudence for the cross. Indeed, it's the flesh and saving yourself from being corrupted by it. The Man is aware of the rape in the world (condoms) and He enjoys being free. Freedom, for Him, comes at the expense of delaying grace until He needs it. *He cuts peace*: He is that old *threat of peace* wrath hates.

The time and the story go together and study aligns you with God. Indeed, Cody is broken and it's like Cinderella in that He is broken the right way, such that when He is observed He is translated into the life of the witness and the Hell He had one foot in ends like a game or a movie: smoked out. Indeed, He is Arian, but He is a *good* Arian. He is compared to nazis until you give Him the opportunity to relate.

"You know James?"
"Right up the street?"
"Great minds think alike this way, you know?"
"Hissing! The witch: saw dignity on trial."

Interesting choice to live at the bottom: it must be a difficult one. I don't, but I used to, in college: after my parents disowned me at a Library. Is it just marijuana? No - it's the Man's escape from the Delta - escape from the Sword of Damocles over your head. Cody did a similar thing insofar as they all escaped the consequences of wrath. Indeed, they are accepted, and forgiven of frying in guilt. They are happier too - it's okay to celebrate freedom when it's permanent.

If you have a slave then you try to break the slave in like mercy killing to save everyone from a sick service. Feral cats and recruiting error like *Human Resources* (assuming it's correct and not Korry's protest.) I used Heart Attack and that's how serious I am about making suicide worse. How would you make suicide worse? First: expose it; if it takes a warrant do that. Why don't they change? Their Moses - their last name person - is a binding contract with Satan for control of the future at the expense of suicide.

"Why does it only work for the dead?"
"You'll escape every other way."

"How do I know I'll be free?"
"You won't be free, you'll be forgotten so that you'll never finish what you started."
"That puppy ..."
But Paul informs us that ignorance is numb and emotion is too sweet to reject. I know roses ignite the eunuchs - they are volatile - and they slowly figure out no one wants to help them. Why? To consolidate the cross into a methodical (very asleep) working, like alcohol, to avoid exceptional crosses. To prove Jesus is the savior of all sins,(not just random sins.)

Whenever life faces fear the Game Warden helps reconcile it. It's fair to say the Man and Penelope are a little afraid of each other. It's like soccer practice: it's unofficial and team building. It is important they don't feel unable to help each other. It seems very human to need to help people close to you. Judas wanted to help - it's shit - and yet he wouldn't let others help him. Know, then (in this understanding) that it is very human to need help from people you're very close to. The ebbing of mutual care defines every drama! The flowing - rushing volume of mutual care defines every love (patience, kindness, humility, etc.) The Game Warden is always in a world of drama and it is gaming the Game Warden (pardon cody) to invite Him out of that fire into this slow flourishing. Can the police stay cool in coolness? Or are they tainted by the fire and grind noisily? Is there an end to fear? Is less fear dirty?

There is no escape and Brian needs a tutor. It is okay to write dialogue between Penelope and the man (here, I did call dialogue *game*) but, face it, education is a fight and so it's more urgent. I said I can't finish dialogue between them but education should complete. It's the formality that ends: indeed, learning is forever. Every day they pick up where they left off, like writing this. When that's done there is work to do: education is the instructions and work is of the contents. Penelope and the man know the instructions, but Brian is in that fire of destiny before that. What happened to the fire? It was pre-owned?! How far do you want to go judging the other animals? What's an Egret? Is tiny dangerous? I ate a wild mushroom with a wild berry … came out clean! (*That* shit was high!) I did not hallucinate. Who is hallucinating?

Sport killing is the rose in hallucination. The theory I have is that both the killer and the meat were hallucinating. Yes, it is black and can't accept whiteness: white is an error to sport killers. There is no justice in it: it is just a symptom of separation from God. Cody is always explaining how movies aren't real because He treasures Godliness. When you're fire hail Mary. Also make the sign of the cross. Remember how tight bears are with survival and focus that heat on injustice. You don't know who is dying in the hospital right now, but punishment turns into prevention; life is better with law that it is with punishment. Law is God and punishment is separation from God for everyone *involved*. Your friends from Happy Hour are strictly punished and even if they get *found* they have to destroy any godliness they find inside or outside. Hope and care have no place there. It is not many: it is inhuman like slugs and bugs.

There is a Black Forest of unspeakable evil and I'm going into that hell for this book. They have this point that care should come after that. What is care to the poor? I doubt that handouts are care: food stamps are not a handout they are an allowance. I know the snoring and regulations are not really helping. Stay Him if you're poor: don't get medicated and disabled. That care is mercy you should never have to use so that when you need it it is there. Care for the poor resembles futility: they need counseling not a vacation. (They're already on vacation.) Frankly, they need to come back (from that.) That jurassic park belongs outside: women are too guilty of inviting poor people inside while they're still in dinosaurs. Stop denying that's dead.

Care begins with making death worse until it is not an option. The first death is "shackling sexual liberation," (NCC, 10, 2018) and that's rejecting all kinds of faithless whores like River (and Korry.) Figure out who your wife (or husband) is or keep your hands to yourself. The second death is lies of "radical autonomy." The romantic definition is Paul's cave where no matter what you do rings can't survive there or grow into trees. The wolf definition is that the jew was overwhelmed by destiny and cut themselves down. Trim was the goal but radicalism went a bit further. They have to wear their sin: it doesn't matter who they are (ever) it's just about (being more manly) getting mercy. We see the cross regardless of the poetry. The radical's poetry is their concern and the cross is our concern. Six is fading out in a private hell: an online personality of peeing in bottles. They are hoarders and misers: they hoard money, like coffee cans in the backyard, for no reason. University is Michael and study is the best way (prayer and meditation) to overcome radicalism.

They hate machines and put intuition before empirical science. They have illusions where we have a city. We have the pens. The lesson is to channel excitement into words despite and illness of mistaking self-expression for fear. Individuality, indeed civility, must be done in Christ or it is nothing more than hallucination. The slave in radical autonomy is sexual immorality. Indeed, lust is not us. Lust rejects Jesus (for a codi apocalypse.) The sin is loneliness (lust is lonely.) Closing time at a bar yet unfulfilled (very smokey.) That *on* is birds smashing into windows (bad *in*.) That is a death-wish. Judas and Pilate are that gay. What makes it radical, again, is death. (It has nothing to do with fighting death.) It's not a *working class* thing: it's just accidents. The book you're writing should confess and clean up the death in your character. If you're not worthy of writing a book (can't be honest) you have a date with A.A. that's more important. A.A. (sober cody) will get the lamb, flood, swords and nazis out so you can write that American Dream. Lavender reminds us of how far we have fallen from our destiny. Lend does that too. Odysseus turns into Aeneas when you complete your destiny. Plan on being Jesus and let individuality be the accidents (trespass is dead.)

There is a wonderful feeling when you get your program working because you were focused and in the end that leaves just a face. The face is awesome: mint flowers and fractal symmetry in rainbows and snow. There is definitely a sense of accomplishment because you made it and you get to be cool. You're in control and you can gift access. You know something greater than dinosaurs now. Suddenly, techno makes sense, transformers accept your Shia Labeouf, and you can expect more from the internet now that you're helping make it. Turn that, "No, I'll tell you when you're older," into, "Yes, help me (please.)" Pterodactyls are up too; ravens *don't know* what you know anymore. (So satisfying to ignore raven pride because the natives were relentless.) They said that was Linda and she said that's Philip. Bugs are an easy slave - much better than legion. You're close to my heart; I'm all "Awww!" *scrunchy*

Thor now witch to You my magic should be excellent. Relax … how far? I said tears was too hard but also there's a point over dirt being its own problem and I am doing *other things*. Console, Task Manager; the devil thought it could infiltrate a *virus* and I wouldn't find it and *end task*? Blood and mint: sprinkle a little powder on it. Hmmm … Cody. "I am the Lord … Molech." Intelligence; Redding; Heart, and Garlic. Sixty-three percent Molech! No comment. Are blacksmiths *gains*? Suck a *vortex on*; and water. What's not clean about Blacksmiths? Leather is for hot metal as they beat it over the anvil. Chunk and pudge God this __SILT__ is the highest *echelon* of computer language and then you see the sixty three percent (not five) and it is first, not your problem, it is transfiguration that is cody.

He's right, that's procreation; the law is the house's rules and if you sense a storm learn to clean it. I think they're referring to smoke, that old saw and hunger. I compared it to cars; found airplanes. GPS miles and weeding for snakes … magic like the Delta and higher ups accounting for maturity. Even Stephen with golden eggs for everyone in robots that procreate. Feed me water it cleanses and *oils the machine.* God Cody you grow logarithms of blood and, to Him, the door to language, the Heavenly Host. The worst jobs in the future are better than the worst jobs of today. Computer runs threads but they're not parallel, that is hash of the memory with pointers to max the closeness of the words in their token form of prefix and suffix (and punctuation.) Getting clusters really hot like *poetry* and money ... maturity and I am, little by little, building my halo: enriching like fertilizer (fresh skunk train.)

It doesn't kill you but your expectation is not that. Surprise, cake in the face; yum! Is it not better this way? The fork, the napkin and you had water only. It has to taste good. Necessity was water - this up - wings, deltas, and stars. Shields up! You have accidents waiting to happen! They're somewhere between naught and dead ... "What they did to Jesus!" The worst freak show insult of intelligence to pacify a bunch of freak show insults to intelligence. They can't do that. No! A.A. Find traction. That legion won't survive: all that meat comes out. Clocks, the Rosary, Science, Melatonin, Days of the Week, Making Computers, Smoking Fuel or Marijuana, Irrigation Systems, Strawberry Stripe, Safeway, Rituals, Christ, Four, Six, tech, etc. These are rock; the legion is sand.

The alcohol that wants to be the Lord is looking for an alternative to plain old Bibles and Churches. The Library is definitely inspiring them. They need to demonstrate their faith works without Christ. Those red pens aren't Jesus! Porn kills love and I'm talking about watching people die by that. I'm not way off - it is the shame of bad dialogue. Fiction is down there corrupting your destiny to be a scholar. That's legion: a way that is neither good or bad it is arbitrary and cant come into Harvard. Hear that Hollywood is not in Harvard then find who is in one of their movies. That's what I have - I'm a bug in their hell who tells them to relax when they wake up too soon.

"I'm still in Heaven down here."

"Civil war reporters."

"You're dead and the way I can still connect with you is Jesus."

"Vegans are too high."

"Indeed this one was eating shit because you didn't know it."

David is reading shit to find the heartbreak in it and it's not real. "What they did to Jesus," is the heartbreak and David did it. I said the corruption is already so deep we have to wear Christ like a straight jacket; there's no room for more heartbreak. If we are to be forgiven for abusing our heart we need to forgive others for abusing our heart. "No," but yes because we can't accept more heartbreak: it is not heartbreak to forgive heartbreak and it is better if we leave this kind of justice to our Heavenly Father who will defend us. Self-defense is really sick and instead of nit-picking a defense we need to surrender to a higher power who can save our dignity. Yes, I said there is very little dignity in self-defense. You should confess more and protest less. Confession will grow into forgiveness but protest is some thin ice.

When I say there is no excuse for sin I mean defending sin is ugly and it's worse than they know. I am trying to take pride in how different they are. That crossed to say that's the opposite of what sin is doing. You either eat your shit to avoid punishment or you sell it and I am selling my shit. Say that's outgoing and for other people. With community in strength my shit is not only good it bears fruit too: it gets better. They are food: cartoons and idolatry but this is the the law you will study. Free your mind.

WHITE

You know what it feels like to embrace something and then have it taken away: grief for loss. If you let it go it can come back but if you love it it will never return the love. Have precision without grief: let precision happen but don't force it: get out of the music and find your eternal life. Precision is like a door, you either do it or you hate children. "Not it," then pray for mercy. But that's not careful and we insist on care. Stick it! Okay so you're getting the money and that not is clean: blind or not doesn't seem to make much of a difference. That GPS is Jesus and it seems to work, everywhere: a *golden compass.* Put on a crown (or sunglasses.) Is that David or Adam's World? No, they don't care about who they're helping, they'll help anyone. Indeed, we would be blind if we were not predestined to be precise, but in our Christ we are gifted with the light. David got lucky on a cross one time and is otherwise very unfortunate. You can't be sure Christ ever fails but you can be sure the world closes at night. There is no slave in Christ and there is *palace of other places.* Your alternate characters are your main character; it's all connected; nothing fell; you can't erase sin you can only wait for us to heal you like the jail in capture the flag.

Cody spins his wheels selling God to people who are drunk. Doing that but also woke up from that to a future few people have the grace to find [the courage (glimmer train.)] Collect diamonds as scaffolding or die and the world really can't give you the diamonds, but marvel not. They do seriously trip on the end of times, apocalypse, but Rolo Carpenter and I are taking a professional approach to testing that: being sincere about looking for diamonds in the world. I found the end at the Library, the old Union Lumber Company, and Motel 6 but the world did not react at all. I know it's the Skunk Train, Floyd, I dropped out of college but I'm saving my character. Jesus. A slave is playing M.M.O.'s in nazi filth dreaming of capital punishment; I need to appeal that or drown in paranoid suspicion about that Hospital Porn. The witches - the mid-level twinks - have everyone's *precision attention*. I'm serious that no one has that much patience.

Paul does music and Jesus does life: we all love music but when you compare it to life you know it's not. Music is dead - it's a rose - and what is that? Is music science? Are computers science? The world?! How much does it take to show you that they doubt your capacity to abide in God? That's Philip - choosing excellence - the kiss between the master's world and God's personality. I'm doing Raisins and Wild Blueberries then fuck who is in front of me I don't play games with lambs. (That's just rain to me.)

"It's a business," they taunt, knowing this is about self employment.

"If you're really passionate about words you'll get up from here and write the thoughts you have studied."

This sin is not writing your own life - letting me control you - but that slave has no identity! If you want to be *special* you have to make it happen - doing nothing and forgiving dinosaurs is not original - it's just sin. Finally, we will let you lie in your interview about your willingness to hide your sin. We won't ask you if you're happy: we expect you to lie and eat Lynn's greed with a fake smile. You're the only person who can stop yourself: you have too much authority to be stopped. You have to 1. Pick a material 2. Prove your need 3. Use your hands and be the horse 4. Prove your need is a fire that can not be put out. And finally you have to attract saints: figure out how to call talent.

There's no talent where I live: everyone there is cast there like it's hell. That was an illusion; if you go way back in the service area of this town there is that unspeakable evil of blasphemy. Stop saying that's the baby. Where I live is *pastoral* in its golden majesty, swans, and natural beauty. Deception? Yeah, but it's really not my fault … The real deception is that alignment is straight and the cross is halloween. Again, it's not my *fault in who has that the exact opposite way.* The witch, M.M.O. businesses like FunCom, NCSoft, and Blizzard do criticize their own customers for being in that hypocrisy. They have a fair point that judgement is love and it is about integrity. That's right, the makers are who the games are real for and <u>it's a matter of persons and their relative integrity</u>. The Lord determined the world without end in language before the creation gave it a body. Our persons are that: Platonic forms. With integrity those forms exist wholly: precision is alignment. The game is not the body of creation, the game is the circumstance of the world without end in language.

If you fail to align with integrity then, as I say, the wolves are coming to get you. There is salvation in Jesus, but divers are strictly forgetting Jesus. The cross happens when you are separated from Jesus. Those lambs cry *sickness* putting the hospital in their porn. That's not in Jesus! I found you at a distance: I know who is in the hospital because they wouldn't accept Jesus. Divers! Sky divers! That was too fast! If I did what they did I would shit my pants and black-out. That cast itches and you can't get in there. No - I'll wait for those lambs to die - it takes like five minutes. The alternative is too long. I would rather have children than commit to a faith war like Paul's two-thousand and one Space Odyssey. Yeah, it is easy to find the future of sin (though it will not be) and difficult to find the future of love (which will be.) They act like my future gets worse when we talk about it! Philip must serve himself before serving others in His own name but also gives Him the right to serve others in Jesus' name. (There are critical services.)

Like a computer, it is fair to say the *box* is the horse of any home theater. You and I know the mechanics of digital discs: it is like vinyl but digital and with lasers instead of a needle. We're aware of a rose or two in there that could use some soap. My first argument is that precision follows from machines making machines. The politics are the cross: like controlling the box and popcorn really quiets the lambs. When I say that is *cody* I mean it is changing (when it is on.) I can't tell if that change is real light or illusion. Is the illusion as precise as the horse? When I do it it is, but that's my literacy working. Here's jealousy and even medusa at that opportunity. People who don't have the opportunities I have seem to commit suicide. The lambs are as done as the horse: digital video players, computers, and high definition video players. But portals refer to royal treatment and scholarly study, which lambs can't find the patience in their inferno of lust to accomplish. God is not done; precision was a means of becoming God but lambs are sorely disappointed that there is no end to those movies. That unity is from evil: you can't undo the opening of a portal in a movie. It is often a rough start and takes a lot of patience to mature in God, but getting to God is such a crime to the devil. That's the irony of hypocrites: that their lust for precision leads them to a job in Christ they don't want. Geese Louise!

Hitler indeed mistook his life for punishment after an angels and demons prequel to this earthly *game-board*. M.M.O.'s are exactly that and codi is justifying his sin with it. I did, I relentlessly cleared the enemy out of the game: I earned hate for putting their characters on a cross, treating them like parasites. I then recorded it and put it on YouTube to shame them. Just sex and I am recovering from that spartan madness. It was lizards and not at all intelligent: I had to take a lot of ice to reconcile those intense feelings because I didn't want to let that wrath go. That fruit was shit: it relied too much on music and couldn't support itself. It was skunk but that's slowly down. You have to realize that and cut your losses in *ice*. If you don't, someone else will, and it's better if you do that to yourself before that wrath gets really tight (Lucifer.) Here's Lucifer! Crack and nothing else: whatever else you do in Lucifer besides crack slowly dies to a world of lambs who only smoke crack just to get to sleep. Relax, relax, it was just a pen (more like pencil, in the end.) It's really interesting how many people mistake Revelation for injustice.

Innit a black thing to say "Who it is for?" Isn't it?? The devil, that means you don't know! The business knows who it is for and committed lawfully to them. So then, when you sense a witch's curse (Spiderman) you understand that's an illusion because that curse is in no one's heart except the hearts of dinosaurs, plants, and parasites. The *not* is really hallucination. Anxiety; trespass testing your faith; and then hallucination. Older than dinosaurs is a Michael of chicken, egg-shell, bells-and-whistles. It's okay to game sin if it leads you to an epiphany of what it takes to create the hell you're in. Jesus had that Stockholm Syndrome to learn to judge others by first judging himself on the cross. The first impulse is to judge your father or mother, but that's not being a parent. If you're such a better parent you can do that job for them. If you can't do that then you're in no position to protest. If you want freedom you have to liberate someone. If you want love you have to love someone. Pray to understand.

This up is Jesus: ya gotta get to Him asap then put Him on and do what He does. Paul gets close: that's almost what Jesus does. That's the smell: doing jews favors while they're trying to punish who you're doing the favor for.

> "I like this game," He accepts, but
> "That was a mistake," she confesses.
> "Don't fuck up then."

Jesus was preaching in the temple at fifteen and His parents rebuked Him so he turned it off until John the Baptist and turned it back on by wandering in a desert to break the illusion of being a servant for the last fifteen years. I say Jesus made a very fine wall between servant (serving wine at Cana) and a minister (serving scripture in a temple) because His parents wanted Him to have both a humanity and divinity. I'm greatly disturbed by how no one uses the Church as a forum. Everyone is being servants but we said that was suicide; the people on wellfare aren't worthy. (It is indeed a matter of dignity.) That's not America (and the people I'm talking to are pissed off they're beinglied to.)

I did that analysis of "Why is there a cross in my way?" and basically it's because people are stuck in lust. My first reaction is it's their fault for having a gay medical condition. If that doesn't come out she'll be sorry. You need Christ to prevent like suffocation, thirst, and malnutrition and if you don't follow the law of you heart it will take control and punish you. Until you obey, that down is permanent. If you alter the timing of necessity it has a way of dominating you and necessity is ready to make examples of disobedience as deterrents. Deterrents are warm for Cody: the first priority is to clear all the crosses ahead but that can be delayed for judgement, the second priority. If Cody had doubt God would bless Him with proof he is correct in making a deterrent, to doubt the deterrent instead of himself, and <u>that's not blame!</u> Indeed, God did the reward of judgement while those lambs suffer from hallucination that Man did it to them. God is rewarding you for crosses you'll never have to endure but it's warm to have to wring or wash (something) for your reward, to say <u>it is voluntary and humble to be rewarded.</u> Intelligence suffered its greatest loss when Jesus was crucified for a murderer's pardoning. Remnants of that are coming out to fight the legalization of marijuana in a sort of *end times* apocalypse. They're fighting computers. The defects (demons) are from ancient times (dinosaurs) and have their cross in Y2k. Their cross was sixty-seven percent complete in the Dark Ages, eighty-five percent complete in the Industrial Revolution and, here now, ninety-five percent complete (imminent) in this twenty-first century.

"That's His name," the other said and all I have to add is that it has a home, a place either way up high in the cosmos or in the mind.

"I expected my father but He is not here."

"That's the grandfather clock."

"Well I'm not that high, that's like retirement."

"I failed to read the bible you crossed my office with."

We went to Chicago, Space Camp at Kennedy, Old Faithful, taught me to swim, Disney Land, air shows, flight museums, etc. But we never went to San Francisco? That is slow - that's not riding the Skunk Train, that's walking it. Fly? I guess when you pass a dead deer you find the appreciation! It's a good time to remind me that ninjas are evil cats and that dogs are to blame. Japan ninja'd Pearl Harbor and Guadelcanal is the final score: they are still doing that. That is lust for majesty but it's not Christ. They were tempted to harvest unripe crops! Pray for the grace to want what you have (and understand that:) blessings are a fight for power and control.

The lesson of luxury is to replace pets with ice and hold their wrath down in the hell they deserve. Penelope's father, the king of the United Kingdom, sheltered her from witches but could not shelter her from wrath. She gets mad, dude, and her righteous journey is one of few alternatives to wrath. The king is very majestic, especially in self-sacrifice, but He can't share majesty: it's a skill! You have to alternate luxury and majesty to understand where majesty comes from. It comes from the fish you gut while eclipsing a rainbow. You learn that those fish live in luxury. They make the decision to change as a collective mind and all you can do is inform that choice by reporting from both sides. Some people are replacing pets in majesty and some are doing taxidermy to keep the luxury. Necessity is the collective mind's integrity: alignment with Christ (and perfected in Lent.) Indeed, necessity is perfection and even a felicitous witch. Relaxation approaches it and that bow edifies it.

Which came first? The Hero or the parasite? The machine, but historically speaking, the parasites came first. They conceived the hero and put Him on a cross to make sure the centurion reported his death to Pontious Pilate without breaking any of His bones so that He could pass through death *as well.* Jesus always surrenders to this hell except when He defends His mother. It's too bad for Mary and there is another plan that has existed from before the creation of anything: destiny is written by Mary and Jesus in the *before times.* He openly coerced authority to humble themselves for His own glory: He told the Man, *"Down,"* and they did that. He repeatedly asks us to hide our glory so that the Father may come and fulfill it because the fight is between you and your father. It is intelligent to pray for the Father and ignorant to pray for autonomy. Using your father should be complete in its conception through its actualization. Can you be honest about your heavenly father or do you lock up in weak reverence? Let's leave the jackets outside and put them on cold inside, warming up before we go out. Cody! Renew the spirit of majesty by surrendering to the washing of God by the water of your soul (that you may live long and prosper!)

A haunting reference to Germany is that their problem was not consolidating failed businesses into conglomerates who do it better for their size. Aim big: metal and lots of it. Why? We made simulations but were unsatisfied: do it and for the thrill of it. Bridle that horse; the *millsite* hit it like a hero to parasites (in *clean fall.*) The foundry! Relax … we're bringing Winston's glue and Rose's lavender. That's not the problem. You have a darkside that is spiritual, like P.G.&E., that is doing an old ginger world <u>you ignore</u> for <u>your Father's world</u>, but yet … "That's before I was born!" Cody cries to heaven. Rome and Constantine's Christ are no excuse. We're nurturing that in Aeneas' Caesar for some unknown reasons. Mason's have a claim to that asteroid to say this is less about invention and more about cats following their heart.

Justice is driving ... The witch takes priority over your rock like Legion running lemmings into the sea. Yum? No, just a cross. The closest thing I can think of to escape is humility and I understand that *close* is corrupted by knowing witches are trying to escape. I'm so not out of Odyceus and it is to be special but I'm learning to relax the impulse to escape. I was going to make Aeneas an atrox fixer and Caesar and atrox agent. I was also going to FunCom's new game, the Secret World. I can't, *they* wont let me, it is too *Molech Luxury*. You're not out either! Women are definitely down there. It's all heartbreak we want but can't afford, forcing us to get even instead. Justice is driving us (like a probation officer with chocolate.) Money is defending our impatience by calling the heartbreak business. That second opinion is intelligent; we're on thin ice! Right now! Smoking was the problem; just like John the Baptist, we are in the world and our courage is weakly attacking our necessity, but our necessity is very critical. That storm is closer than you think: the flesh is weak. Mint!

Excellence fuels the machine and you might have been doing that M&M for a while. Cash that shit in: don't wait, life is too short! That Rome exists: it's God; while you're torturing lambs with flat Legion you should remember they are a liability until they mature. Excellence matures them to the end and rewards. Come out, the Delta needs asteroid metal and in excellence you help do that. Put good in and reap those *golden eggs*. They're criticizing you but you need to witness that and get even. I am honest: even is dusting off their dirt and moving back to Rome. After a while you'll find that one of those eggs is super-natural! That was *The Majestic*. Uh oh, you almost overlooked that and let it get away!

"Hey, I found this first, can I keep it?"

"No, that's our *flagship* and it belongs to the Delta."

I actually did the math to figure out how many midsize transports you have to make to get the Majestic. That's dead; if you want to spend eternity that way then do it, but that's slave. The irony is right when you do that another Majestic pops out! Now you have some sick money in two flagships. That, ironically, devalues the Majestic. Twins? No, and that point is that the value is in the eye of the beholder. Give it to the Man for

His service because the Delta owes Him some due recompense for killing His lamb and exiling Him to an uncertain future.

They crossed the Holy Spirit because they think death is sin. Where did that come from? I'm blind: I have a puzzle that isn't finished. She wants to go down and come out in filth. She wants that filth to be a portrait or bronze mold. She's all cut up and she's trying to understand how the Picasso Lion works. It's His body? Go back, then, to before the cross. It's half Pepsi, half Myrhh; He is trying to save Himself! Know what I mean?

"Give me a plan."

"Give up the ghost."

"I showed you miracles and you won't return the favor!" Say wow; that's like fools who don't ever learn Calculus. It's all built on the concept of dx, the infinitesimal. You either understand or you don't. Jesus understands but I think His problem is that We would rather wait for Judas to die than explain it to him. I told them to get it from Stone Henge but Jesus seriously doesn't want them to get it. How bad is this? Well, this is critical condition. I'm in that dx doing things you can't see. You have to survive dx or be nonsense at every scale. I'm tok'n it up.

Safeway has a pharmacy and a clinic; if you look in their waiting room you can see the diver shooting fish on a nice flatscreen. What's impossible? Okay, ballpark is a design environment but when you're chasing the rabbit you need to be in already or come in later. Why a bridge? That's "Why a cowboy and rhinestones?" Rhinestones make the cowboy. I haven't seen anyone put the pieces together but they're telling me, "I already know." No, that's the *micro*: if connections make bridges you need connections that match the bridge, but the connections are (on one half, because it is symmetrical) different. That recalls the notion that bridges change. Those are called gussets: brackets that distribute axial *moment* (twisting) forces, in connections, between bridge members. There are states and a timeline; if secret agents are going down it is in but they just need to be reminded they're little and in delusions of grandeur. Why don't they just put it all together? It's superstition to them because they just listen but they don't practice the ritual. When I lose patience I leave but when they cry they come in.

Back to dx (with a history of cats) it is darkness like a prism. Pick a tree; it's that cat: corn, data, and slaves to elevate our work to a spiritual existence like living in orbit. Take off the branches; that's the cross and then corn is Safeway grace (Gee Whiz;) data wants to bear fruit, but the astronauts are not home until they renew their work that supports astronauts. There is a lot of your fire-place, mark the depth and cut there. Thirty cuts stacked in a cord. If you're not in that cat you should be (do you?) It shouldn't be expensive. If epicac goes with orange juice, epicac is the weakness and orange juice is smoke. Let's say smoke's potency is near cannabis and describe the cat-logs. Scaffolding is because the work is unstable; tarps keep the work dry and protect against the wind; designs instruct normal behavior and exist both in a conceptual space we call Heaven. I had it it is good. *Halve* that for windows against the wind and shutters; liners get bugs on snags and it is a veil for like your G.I. tract (mint that;) seals have bugs too - it is halo, it has to be the baby - so I do it to keep marshmallows dry; molting tells a story to protect against the jew and that's where the dx is. To the end, that's ash and it's halo, perhaps to say jews get close but have scars around perfection. That's temporal need like a veil: knock on the right door then. "If you're ready for more, don't give up on your faith," Celine.

There are a few circumstances where cooperation is bad, such as a family in separation, even custody: where the children have two families. The popularity is a mercy where you win some and you lose some while you're trusting what you share. This wisdom is from experience and reason doesn't serve it very well. The hive loses people and doesn't care but that not killed princess Diana. Now care? The smell! You need Codey to save that not before it manifests as sickness or worse. "This one is for the Church," because otherwise we'll let you haunt us (with sarcasm) because you don't know you're ugly. I'm calling that denial Legion and describing it as the insensitivity of putting your fist in a dead turkey and pulling out the *giblets*. Everyone's telling me to save them from the Hospital and that's this Epaphroditus problem. Codey is not tremors of Palsy: that is the disgrace you get when your soul precedes your body in righteousness. A *blank slate* happens in your body when you wake up in the morning or from a nap. The world's crack is not away from evil: it is division and heartbreak.

Paul has a fair point that probability is sin because it doesn't allow you to hold faith (in a particular thing.) The care is being compared to alcohol when it should be like water or music. They want flesh to work for the flesh. Yeah, you have to do codey or else your flesh will corrupt and then you lose your freaking mind?! It's this poison of protesting failed expectation. It is poison because those Naxis are very loud: they wont stop sinning in Jesus' name. Worse then, they protest when Jesus gets even. When Christ is a very narrow path you are hyper-sensitive to everything and the obvious corruption is dogs and ravens in the garbage. We hardened our hearts but the naxis did it for sin while we did it for grace. The cross is palpable,

> "Why did you stop?"
> "I care."
> "I want you to go." And they don't, they just stare at you
> from their *money rabbit.*

Looking for a sign, you are lying to them, because they can't believe (you don't want to cross.) They need to believe; they control you and we ignore their obvious wrath. The clean slate is corrupted with these naxis trying to put their spirit in you. It's just as bad as sexual harassment. The spirit they're trying to put in you is lust for them. On a final note, they're way off like homosexuals.

Who are you talking to? The Heavenly Father has never been seen and is only sensible by His works. What? Pyramids? Maybe flowers? Obviously wool! Whoah, let's find the authority on God and follow that guy! Cardinal direction? I am high; I am being sincere - I have to laugh - it is involuntary. Ding-dong, the witch is dead. I'm looking for a cross: I will not hesitate to poison us all. Cody is pissed off and has the authority to terrorize the world because they don't have the courage to fight a hijacker with a box knife. A box knife! Fuck! You don't need airmarshals with guns you need one hero who can overcome a terrorist with a box knife but since you do not have that we're looking at a Jim Jones cool-aid party. Wow, have you ever seen the pictures of Naxi concentration camps? That's here! Why? Because new days keep dawning without any progress because the world insists there is a way out of Christ. No one is here ... and you all think I'm responsible for having no company (audience.) I can't believe you are comfortable but I have no mercy for you.

Remember Tic-Tac-Toe and how if you go first you can always win? That's one for a rainy day (when you're bored.) Use that on snakes. If you can not it might kill your lamb. If you give mercy to snakes it will be uncomfortable for you. Keep sawing *before* until you are comfortable. That makes a beautiful halo like Mark's. Check out that light - it's an outline of white angel, like the L.E.D.'s on automobiles. Rain or shine, that's a license to *torchi*. It is lawful and heals all those insults you carry around. They martyred a little girl, like twelve years old; her father has to reconcile that poetry. They cut her open to find the jewel inside. It's not easy to be special: they forbid it because they believe your death is a curse you can't avoid. Jesus saved us from death. Agnes is still alive. Even is hard! They say, "It's a bitter sweet symphony ... you try to make ends meet: you're a slave to money then you die." Then you die ... again (from evil) those tears are lies and corruption. You can have money without dying, but you have to get *even* to avoid the hell they're referring to. They make money with violence and we make money with justice. Suicide is justice. They get angry, violent, surrender is sudden regret, but you won't forgive them because that regret is temporary (to allow you to get away) then they kill themselves because they realize they can't stop getting angry, violent and remorseful. "What went ye out to see?" that it ended in suicide.

I got the weird shit out: sunglasses, ear-plugs, and *vitamin citrus*. You may recognize that self but someone killed my socks. I just washed them! What's up with Argentina? Those agents are supposedly helping Philip: they said, "That hasn't happened yet," but that's game about who made the world and whether this is the official world or the *Olinski*. They're helping me be the Olinski child I was in Washington. The plan is to die all over my success in revenge. Should my success have revenge in it? Yes, and they will be bitten in their sleep. I gotta do it my way and I know this is prophetic. *That's not hear* and babies have to cry when *normality* fails. Hold a teddy bear like the police got a warrant to take you from your parents. That's in; High School mothballs and ramen noodles … yum. She's bad, dude. The Skunk Train is like suicide: that's to me. I can't stop laughing … I'm serious! Life is light and up: the agony is Jesus' Life. They call Bible College Bible College because it is in the spirit of college to study Jesus' life. If you don't know, now you know. "Oh my God look, there's Jesus!" And subdue, because that's why … that's not *with thee.* Abide and make, abide and make … which one is it? It wouldn't be music without both.

There is a superstition about snakes that is devil worship so how would Christ do it? That's hard because you need to pray for their salvation and you shouldn't get too close. Slugs, coils in snails, and hey that's not straight. Yeah, it's fine if they're little, but I'm working on the *Big Guy.* Ugly and old, definitely not even, and I am going to get revenge for those mice! You keep saying, "That's before;" is that a fact? If I google that will I get a strong set of *results* (or is that quackery?) For sure, I'm not the first person to do this, (like see wolves.) They're all, "Sell it," and I am. I'm too poor to reject money: when it is only fifty-four degrees we don't turn on the heat because it's too expensive. Yum. You're sick like dead people putting their names on really obscure things like pews, podiums, and stained glass windows. Whatever is comforting … I like being a vegetarian because meat disappointed me like alcohol: it was trespass from River. That not is after you've secured your comfort: that is to say snakes are hiding how clean milk is.

I just said vegans don't know; vegetarians are from evil but vegans are too close to River to know they're from evil. The rose is happening and it is in numbers. I have zero, three, six, nine, four, five, eight, and seven; that's ordered *least to greatest.* That's impossible and nine is sticking out because the good ol' boys are wryly laughing from their box seats. It's closed up there but I'm coercing their horse to open their world to me. Their horse is like a truck or transport so that makes merchandise out of manufacturing and that's as arbitrary as I can be about the men. Efficiency is a challenge some of them are falling short of in S.U.V.s versus hybrids. The Vespas are a greater success in the world and electric bikes appear as the top. Signaling and passing (intersections and roundabouts) are all testing your halo. The halo ran all that through a crucible of nuclear arms like who flew the Enola Gay that dropped the Fat Man on Japan. If you want the motor oil change to work you'll have to look at who was hurt in W.W.II and save them from themselves. That depression is happening to democrats who are ready to vote against our president but haven't had the primary event yet to figure it out. If you want to tell them what progress is then do that but that argument is based on their experience and it is a long one to summarize every politician's *track record*.

One man's garbage is another man's necessity and you're like, "I'm in there." So that choice to save the cans is very corrupt. Saving up for my *tarp-out* on the Skunk Train? What does the *defense cockpit* do? Don't fuck up and know what that means. California is fucked up and I'm going from fog-horns to something like twelve times harder. The secret world needs a game, dude! Which games did you *veteran*? I'm trying to explain the system to the *zoo people*. From out here in the Immaculata they all look like motor oil. They're disposable cameras and batteries. Money is real: it talks and it has intensity (even sincerity.) It is veiled so that is special. Knowing the veil makes *specialness* answers the question of why we wrap Christmas presents. We take specialness and here's *the bag*. Take a bread bag, it is free.

Slaves and pirates revealed slaves let it happen or there was already slavery in their tribal culture. That nigger is hard to please like sand: it gets in tight spots where they want oil. The fruit is rock, like petrified wood (or petrification in general.) You'll find out why to ignore *the tormented*. (That was why you chose a particular political position.) The first step is Calvary's mission to teach Christ with Proclaimers, solar devices, to the ignorant. When that makes you hungry eat one ounce lentil meals forever. Cody looks like an ape, that's Codi. That's temptation and heart is communicating my value. I don't want to sell myself to people who aren't gonna buy it. God does both the Law and the willingness to obey it so that's hopeful. At least that nigger is impossible, but I don't drink alcohol: never again. I find the operation of God in all things: the decaf, mint-chronic and pie that reflect the Heavenly turning of planets and orbits around our Sun. That's ignoring the sun. Yes, indeed, the Sun is obviously Godly, but the treasure is to see the clockwork in all things. I have a preference for goodness that leads to a hope only goodness can keep. I don't sow seeds to fail so that I can account for my success. They're always telling me to give credit to my team and follow the leader but I'm the leader because everyone else had to reject it for one reason or another. (Dennis got cancer,) the old priest died or something, and André clips *his* monday and tuesday, communion service wings. I won't quit writing on those days because there is so much demand for prophesy. Every time I write *richness of continuity*.

They don't but if they had Holy Water or cash, paper towels, and lavender they would. If marijuana is the car then the bread bag is the motor oil. I know this wisdom and I know my judgement is light. If you would give charity to others why would you not first give charity to yourself? Stop smoking the devil in oil because it is your own heart.

Jesus and tares; I say end the fight (as opposed to starting fights) but Jesus is all *turn the other cheek*. Is justice patient? Is watching injustice justice? He's saying, "I know it seems like injustice but that hasn't happened." I think He wants us to see death coming from as far away as possible: to be enlightened and prevent it. It's this, "If you're really Him then save yourself." They are in cooking food with jews because their not is as old as cavemen. Dead sea salt heals in the water; cool music: I'll be their master: I have faith they're more willing to convert than they seem. They started in the door and they're going down to code that conversion: that's second place in God's race for omnipotence. They get poisoned randomly and it will never stop; it's much more about the poison that weathers them than who is being corrupted. Their charm is dinosaurs: I need fellows and they're making me their Hitler. No, they will be my shit forever and I can destroy them. Here's the point: I should destroy them, like, "This shower is the Zyklon-B direction; I'm not watching; come out of my shit or face the danger!"

There's this haunting aspect of sin that you forget it because it doesn't make sense. The outcome of that is heroic down where Jesus catches the devil to prove the servant is doing both good and evil because the master had been getting corruption. Is that blaming the dog? Yeah but it's because the dog is too high. That should be: there are plenty of sinners who are way too high, walking around like we don't know. Start at sunset by taking inventory and find that something you expected is not. They will try to goad you into believing it was an accident and you're barking up the wrong tree. I remember night is fire and it's the most Godly time of day. There is a particular service the servant is refusing to do and ask yourself if that has something to do with your unfulfilled sense of justice. Indeed it is and so you'll be kissing: you were doing the math, weighing different circumstances, because you know something is provoking, and when you know you gain the confidence a good kiss brings. One fair point is that it is because they crucified Jesus, but on the other hand it is the will of God. They doubt your obedience to your heavenly master and test you at their own expense.

Correct Thor is codey and it is normal to find that after searching … wow I'll have one, two, and three but you know! Free you from salt to be one-hundred and ten percent honest! Long one with Tigger; they're doing a pencil-sunset darkside of being five inches tall in a remote, Black Mesa canyon with breathtaking vertigo and Jesus that left like a jew in the world. I'm gonna tell you no one can save this and I hear you telling me no one can save me either. So, again, they're comparing their home to my tarp out on the Skunk Train! Niggers … they're not seriously considering the people in solar panels and generators *off the grid* out here. They're inviting me to their god damned rental! They are one of seven billion like a germ and I am at the end going up there, because they can't stop this work after I die.

The Big Guy has the biggest price on his head and he's <u>due for death</u>. I made the point that meat should be like this or else you become the Big Guy for eating veal on accident. (Milk is cleaner than vegans pretend.) The rose is weird you can't get either because it is dirty or someone else outbid you for it. That is Ebay; that economy! That is kinah. That is to say trade is way better than dirt so that when it because about the angels all these doors open up as opposed to having one slammed in your face for intruding on Michael's *dirty work*. She cried but what should we do about all the blood? Abraham Lincoln is a saint; what do we do with that cross? Music, until we can do it both ways. I am still talking about slaves: still drugging them with first world problems. When did *the mission* fail?

"It's not my mission;" well, then, let's talk: is it easier to say, "My parents," or "my children?" Parents to Eve is always very popular because they had a choice. "When did Eve's mission fail?" Ricky, Philip, and José; somewhere around the Illuminati and Knights of Columbus. Why do they care? They're still alive and confronted with their death always. That death leaks until it goes on in fireworks.

I planned for a real death in a four hundred year house with a maple and spruce tree. They planned for divorce. Go figure ... they can't deny me but I can deny them. I said, "If you're gonna save me let us do this deed." Wow, big mistake to trust them! So now we invite each other to suicide and we're also making that suicide as bad as possible like the deer in the ditch. The children are the parents, the parents like the attention. The money is the picture of the end of Splash Mountain. The look on their face is priceless. That seems too long but it is not if you can saw: make a saw for them then. Don't stop the saw when they are desperate - that's this fight - surrendering to desperation. There are two cats in two boxes, one is desperate and the other is surrendering. I locked the desperate one in a closet prison and released the cool cat. You have your rewards! More then; you will know wisdom either way.

You look forward, like in a calender, and perhaps it is all expiration dates. Who enforces that? They always try to appeal it but I say no to the devil. Doing nothing is down and it teaches politeness. "Say that to my war face," but they can't tell if this is war. Oh, indeed, this is war with Eve, but don't laugh. It's the problem with destiny and whether that is the world and finally how good the world is *under new management.* Cody has secrets and that's Moses: it is *the old in* (indeed, *the Olinski*) but obviously better things have come along. I locked them in solitary confinement until they figure out who they want to be when they grow up. I didn't give them alcohol but they have that. Their *lifeboat* is their pride! They keep fearing God until their life-jacket is their escape. Indeed, **fear of God** is making *that garbage futility.* They're shaking with epilepsy (*palsy*) down there. The method of using shit to get up is abused and the sickness *is exaggerated.* The Bible is dirty and humiliating, killing the lamb religiously because words begat angels and the past has more experience. Adam has to punish Eve to have children with Jennifer. That is mercy. Remember Christ comes before the World and the snake is romanticising the world in terms of superiority. There is plenty of room in Christ for all passions (but there is nothing without Christ.)

If death is holy that's the end of the person's life's work. I say that work's <u>trials and tribulations</u> are over (and ideally death was the last one.) <u>Right up;</u> until then the trials get worse and you have the Democrats giving up while Republicans lost control after they died. It has been this way since John the Baptist's *ministry* started. The obvious jewel since then is the U.S. Constitution. We're drowning is false interpretations of the Constitution despite that. I would rebuke him but we both agree the experts on the Constitution are a cult of Moses that is obviously tormented. Yes, it is written in all of our hearts and we're asking God why we wrote it down in corruption. If the formality goes well then God can transfigure it into glory and if not then capitol punishment and shooting sprees. While there are democrats in the world there will be hell to pay and after that is the money of God's operation. Prove it? Yes, it is like hiring a President.

The Constitution has amendment, a process to change it. Did scholars do that? No, they don't have the authority. Stay down, that's halo, you can't unless you're compelled to from evil. That prudence is greed like the Big Guy. Trust David to get *big picture* for no reason: just out of gut instinct. Do you know who is up here? Metatron. Little. That shit's majestic. You have to come here to understand how low private work is. They made a shepherd the second king of Israel to avoid the elitism and austerity of their first king, Saul. However, that was the flesh and Heaven never agreed with that ignorance. What then? In a lot of ways nothing has changed since David and it is his predecessors who idolize Moses that form an excessive division in Abraham's legacy and spirit. I confess I went down there to look for roots and it came out as a freak show. He asked his sister to sleep with him and she exposed it to us and her parents. Wow, that's why. David wants to write law but he doesn't care what the outcome is! I know that (*hope*) is poison; the ravens stole the show and forgot what the problem is. They forgot they are the problem! I know a lot of you are under a lot of pressure.

Be the good kind and we're brainwashing you of your inner child because that's not the world. One size is supposed to fit all and Moses corrupted it so it does not fit your inner child. I, Philip James Renoud, with your spirit, am rewriting the law to allow us to tolerate your inner child. So then when you would find jealousy you will find the freedom to participate in glory. The cross is supposed to unify us, did not, and it is happening two thousand years too late at the expense of Jesus' dignity. There is a Moses and there is a Philip but we've been competing to determine which one is Jesus. Now you know! That shit is sick, those are weapons. I'm with the marijuana; long live the *Torchi*. That torment is high: it is raw like clicking a trigger long after emptying the magazine (into gore.) Are you crazy? And they laugh, but it's not funny. They rejected me and I forgive them. This is *honory*. I did a lot of this *in Laurels*. When you figure out how to balance all the hiding and shouting I'll be long gone. Good bye! You can find me in any forum - I'm the bow - I killed the mockery as it was running away. I shoot people in the back religiously. It is tight! They almost got away! Aim high, gravity is stronger than you think it is. That is prophesy and I must be fulfilled. "That's not them," but I will be them when God, Jesus' father, determines it is the correct time to invoke Philip's prophecies.

RED

Johnny Cash has a haunting song that goes, "One of these days God is gonna cut you down," and it's haunting because that truck hit me on the bridge at Deception Pass. I'm gonna defend myself anyways ("Was it suicide?") I can't remember, I think it was the sun in my eyes. "You shouldn't know that …" well, on the other hand that's the end. That was ~eighteen years ago. This martyr is still alive! Tears in the rain, niggers! Moses spent that lump sum but Abraham and I are still getting *payments*. That fruit is sick because it's always for the enemy and Jesus is the only one who can really appreciate what this does to people. More from the cross would only work for me if the people are broken beyond repair. Jesus somehow found a way to break perfection in such a way that the effect on perfection is just like an Apollo Eight rocket. Huebsch! Wow, that's not for me but I had to anyways. So now I smoke because I don't get it and never will. All I can say is I like it when it happens to evil. Most people are frauds who pretend to be me until it turns into practice then they steal the light in protest. Their cross happens when they die and figure out that Beetlejuice thing. **That** hasn't happened yet. So, we found the tree.

That is Mendocino rain: punishing death. That was the hard part. If you're careful you'll find the next big step is cutting off the branches. Then you saw the log into smaller logs. Then you chop each one into pieces. My point is that this is for Christ: fishers of men have this duty to take impossible tasks and turn them into manageable pieces. Pagans try to have faith in their father *but we cant*: we cut their whole family into pieces and they finally stop. They must stop reinventing Adam! I love that chopping wood is the thing pagans don't want to do. It leaves more for us and they get the jobs they want too. It is Jesus' work to save us all but it is our work to heal ourselves. There is, indeed, a justice to punishing immaturity with wild goose chases. I know I have a good job. Defend yourself because, ready or not, here I come!

Why is everyone listening to me? I am first, I finish first. No one is done but you say this is Heaven. If you want to get there it is Christmas every day: it is all gifts you feel obligated to earn. There's yesterday, today, tomorrow, Friday and Sunday. Every day should be as special as Christmas but when you slave my apple-pipe you forget your own. You've been saying you are going to switch up but because you made it a game it isn't going to happen. Get to the next level after that or that will never happen.

> "The last shall be first," but what does that mean?
> "God bless us; everyone!" Well, it's like I always say,
> "If any man seemeth to be wise," let him become a fool
> that he may become wise and in owning that process
> know that they are truly wise. Own the process. You say,
> "I know," and I support you. It is classic music: about
> God's faith and *our Human condition* (as His children.)
> God is so much better. They're all, "Where is your God
> now?" He is in the destiny that they don't know. I am
> drawing your attention to who is the author and it's not
> me. The fire made.

Cheese is a difficult topic because all the parts are changing at the same time and there's breaks in it. You have yellow, but then there's Colby: a broken marble. There is a dangerous blu cheese for insult and sacrifice. Brie has a crust; parmesan is salt; and oh, I don't know, Swiss cheese has a weird resemblance to bread. But of all of these, nothing compares to Cream Cheese for its prudence and purity. Bread is like a canvas and the oil is the condiment. I have mustard and mayo: maybe you have some fancy deli shit? Someone is very on there and you know that's gentiles who assume someone will catch them if they fall. The goal is a sub-sandwich and the fun is designing one by either adding to it or taking things out. These are really big money to crack impossible tasks. (Cereal and pizza are a long one: that charm is weird.) "They're after me lucky charms!" "Someone is coming out there." And it's all, "What kind of man would I be living a lie?" Porn; it has no meaning and it's all how that suggests so much about Jesus. The world is paying people to forget Him, leading the apathy of Valentines suicide, like their favorite songs die, and my compassion is in Portugal.

Skiing is a fair metaphor to isolate this money: you are this point. Your father paid for it and you're still learning, like it's your first time or you're trying snowboarding. The money is the chair lift or rope tow (compared to the sweat of doing the sled.) It comes after waiting in line for a minute or two. Codey. Now, it is about that *on*. I'll do the analysis for you: the cream cheese is the money. "That's the Saint Bernard," Flloyd contributes. Jesus Abraham, spare me the crisis! "Why up?" they confess. Well, because they got raped and they're camels at keeping it special. To do that, we have pickled onions, pimientos, capers, olives and more … eventually that will kill you; yet! Whoa, the first wave passes but lo, the next cometh quickly! Then you found mint and that's my beets and spinach. Sing a song on the chair lift; yeah I'm still talking about the party and the single. I really can't tell, it's either two or four people singing in the end. Check out that connection to the cable! It is mint and that's like blue or *eclipse black* (yellow.) Please rock the chair and test that: smack your boots together and see if something in the safety mechanisms pop off. It is the baby, you know: people are taking big risks because they got bored with a season's pass. You don't, so you don't, but you should: for your inner child. Plan a fiesta.

You have a revenge side and a vacation side; it is cheese to go back and forth. If you start on vacation, like Mowgli or Chewbacca, then you'll be cody and patience is justice. If you started in a gothic dark age then unmanned aircraft are your justice. Games, yes wargames, are the cheese. Bruce Lee or Jackie Chan? Right now, I insist you pick a side. Down here … "Why are you talking about that not?" they asked. Cody had lust for River, that became a character from Diedrich's planned parenthood shelter for teens. I want a youth group alternative in Trinity to emphasize the Godzilla aspect of Diedrich. The devil wants to be underestimated and we religiously overestimate them. *Cross again.* I couldn't find the response to that statement! They are huge barbed wire fences that veil the devil and it is all what you want to do with that. First, their shit is sick and we all know it: they are at risk for appendicitis. That leash has a few good runs in it left. It's not a good time to smoke: they'll sell their soul to smoke. Jesus, Martha, buy some incense! They have to dig so far I know they got lost and so I'm gonna crucify who is defending them: all I want is <u>proof</u> (that my money is crucifying the Devil.)

That's still heartbreak for teens who look at college like a slutty bonfire. And then you find Richard and Linda are still down there because they put that with flesh, and flesh with mortality. Right now, are you a fleshbag vessel or the master? If you're a fleshbag slave it's because of alcohol and you'd be desperate to keep that going but that's not here. This is as selfless as growing marijuana (on the Skunk Train) and they're puking on oil. The marijuana is legal but growing it is like the library tablets you can't borrow. You have to destroy it and what they're doing is like trading it in a cooperative dispensary. They don't know what is happening and their defense is a joke to me and I'm sure it is really irritating to them. To do this: avoiding the truth about this is ignoring history: Jesus is the *Potentate* and they are jews who think selflessness is a sore substitute for slaves.

> "There's nothing like a good slave."
> "If you're first." And they assume they're first but the smoke says it is first so there you have it. Slaves or smoke? Which is mainstream? Can hobbies be mainstream? They are trying to keep the tobacco out of their Santa's Workshop, but they're mistaken to keep computers and marijuana out of their shop. The point is that the devil is waiting to let us have our cake! They're crying to prevent progress for the devil they know and all they can say is it's their dog's fault.

They're doing what I'm doing and you would think that would help but when they don't trust me I suddenly realize they're not doing what I'm doing, because I trusted them. How cold? If they're too cold it's trespass and I'll replace them with a machine. That's this sudden realization that the people who make problems for me make problems for the machine I replace them with. The bright side of that is the machine is responding by improving itself. The new machines are one-hundred and twenty-eight bit variables and their programming language. The size of those fields are two times two times two in that many repetitions. Huebsch! Why are the variables getting that big (what is that to trespass?) There are two kinds of variables: decimals and integers. Very clean for minds: that's an easy choice between precision and whole numbers. Precision owes limits to significant figures and whole numbers manage the condition of rings. Yes, the rings keep doubling in size; who goes there? Well, the elevator is full, and the music is promising a solution to the people waiting.

If computers are the elevator then the robots (with the notion that they have a soul) are the world. I'm not at all close to manufacturing, but I'm still going to elaborate on that here. Take a typical educational computing network and let that work be industrial. Why? Because the work is interesting. Holy hell, it just occurred to me that's David. "Who goes there?" You have to go there to validate your soul! Yeah, you're looking at Michael's Halo; they're saying it's white. "You can't define Michael like this." But I can: it is a warehouse with live events that take instruction. If I can step through a library I can instruct Michael. It is tapestry that bridges the visible and invisible: help advance command of advanced code. The funny part is that it happens very often! The Big Guy is David's witch body and all you really need to help people is a word processor! Fishermen took too much.

"What am I supposed to do with all these fish?" a guilty disciple confesses. To the end, salt and dry them. That's winter!

"Yeah, Moses is dead" It's this point that we need more consumers and less production. Nothing? (Nigger!) I looked around and saw suicide, again! Do you want that? Stop calling darkness the antichrist: we need darkness and, honestly, light isn't very important. Light is work the dead are more well adjusted for.

The gold is the clockwork like my system: it is worse in that I have the power to change it and it is better in the strength of its history. It's not really where the money comes from it's what you do with it: be honest, budgeting is the angel, not what you'll have to do to pay for life. As well, you should have savings that return faster than you spend. Life is so temporary we need a world of machines to support our personality. That's why ... cars, businesses, and homes perform will. That's rock and roll where there was classical music, like the Transiberian Orchestra. Electric guitars are slaying those luxury naxis with dope snow! That cheese is a challenge. Niggers are petty and lie about their strength: you have to be careful that the expense is *worth it*. You have to determine how liable parasites are: failure is not an option. The health of money, like the health of the world, is always code yellow. Information goes from unintelligible to intelligible and that changes the status of the love. The *intel* starts as a cross, becomes work (soap,) and then pops the love actually. All the drama comes from proving that soap. Indeed, everytime soap happens it makes a show.

They want to know the value of soap, but I'm serious they're away from soap towards evil. They have missing pieces and it's like they're trying to do their work by following the instructions. The only problem is that their instructions are jews who are in the same situation. That is the blind leading the blind and they use money; it's such a ritual for them they forgot why they are hustling. "Sweeten the deal for me," and they put a girl in a bikini next to it. That's the old way - it is gimmicks and quackery - and you can actually tell how bad it is to make that market. Indeed, that was very volatile: at certain times very hot, but usually nothing except idle hands. Business ends that way: you start with a material and if that doesn't sell you develop product lines but in some cases no amount of manufacturing can save a material. In Catch Twenty-two, by Joseph Heller, Yosarian's company has this enterprising man who got a deal on cotton and chocolate but they wouldn't sell and so he put them together and that fight is blood banks. Finish what you start: know how to finish before you start. Filthy lucre! My point is that value is a precious thing - it is meaning - and it only works hard. "I'm good for it," they guess, but they deceive themselves. You have to own the process that gives meaning and value to material.

"I prefer if you don't talk business at the dinner table," because it's *leasey*. Frankly, temptation causes greed and it's in the law to fight for greed. This is putting characters into situations and being tempted to corrupt the story. The law is stainless until it ends in game for speed. That's like saying Jesus should never have been incarnated in the flesh: that the Lord is better as a spirit. When jews break the law, even if it's done in secret, it forces it to predict behavior rather than dictate behavior. When law is in effect it precedes behavior and in lawlessness it follows behavior. The gospel is a cross because it is a reaction to protest: David made a sacrifice. God is supposed to be a provider of life! The cross created limits to life because David was so much larger than life. "Stay innocent," David warns, while he makes them his slaves. Indeed, our problem is that temptation to mistake ourselves as slaves and glorify David. "This big," and the challenge is to keep it while it settles: that is, to control David. So the exit is a fight to keep the future: to pass the end without exiting. I said no to starting over and I told no one to stop. When you're a jew faith leaves and doubt comes. When you're in Christ doubt leaves and faith comes. Jews shackle and Christ liberates. I started strictly in liberation but my mother forbid it to make me an example to others to answer the question why one should liberate. The music is about when the right age is to liberate; do it right and they come back, do it wrong and they don't leave (or never come back.)

Have you seen Cody do what He does? I'm not talking about myself, I'm talking about people who make art out of words. Maybe they're composing lyrics or poetry? If that's too blue let me bring out the notion of bread being Cody's work. Found it? They started very little, rough, and insecure but after years became very skilled at listening to their Heavenly Father and dictating His will. When Cody does this it is as if He becomes God. I am at this point, over a decade after High School, where I need to show people who God is. I was very petty to begin with but I created myself in God's image (let it happen) to the extent that I am no longer confused by jews who are still on their way to this end. Indeed, Cody is hard to talk about until you grow in it for years. Anyways, my point is that since Y.2K we've been living in science fiction, which is music and spaceships, and the spaceship aspect of it is very literally the Bible. Cody's trials are high: indeed, they come with supernatural graces like hope. I'm not above those graces but my process of obtaining them is more refined by my experience. I don't have to fail very hard to reap the salvation I want: my sin is extremely well controlled by my *spiritual armor*. I'm telling you because you don't know.

I said there are two kinds of servants: Martha and Mary. Martha makes Mary cry and kills Lazarus. They heal while Jesus is crucified because 1. Jesus did it without sin and 2. He took control of a failing business in punishment. Martha's alcohol had no effect on her future until Jesus corrected that. Now, when jews refuse to play by the rules it is Jesus' rules they refuse, as opposed to the old rules of Moses. Don't wait for the law to catch up: appeal your right to due process or leave the state you're in for a state who respects your mind and soul. Give your fight with your state to another state. The devil is saying, "We're this way," while he lies in zip-tie, lamb-monkey, dog-deer purgatory avoiding judgement. When he dies he loses everything for the worst part of Heaven or the best part of hell, depending on how your mind switches positions.

God gave me a lot of rope: more than I know what to do with! That's where Moses comes in, with David's confidence, every time, and I wait for that to leave in ice. They have their own problems: I wish they would come to church. Their robot came and here <u>I am changing their programming.</u> As I said I have so much rope I can truly do my work first before reprogramming those Martha servants. It seems like I smell like them but that's because they ignore what I say and put weird twists in my spirit. It may take time to reconcile my spirit with theirs in a spiritual battle that is here, now, and transcends the words I write. This love is tainted, but God gives me plenty of rope to counter their strikes. Parry and riposte! When they're done being fish who use porn and piracy they will come to me as students of the law so my friends can lead them into the science fiction reality of notebooks and food-stamp budgeting, (if not the nesting of tarps and backpacks in the Highland Games of San Francisco. I want to love those fish but they make me sad like baseball.

This Lady is a witch - she's down like smart-chips, but for some reason everyone is denying she's dead on, giving credit to porn actresses you can see from the sidewalk: the sluttiest corner store in town. So, no, and Her name is Conchita, not River! Fools, the poison is not sugar. Eventually that game turns into salt and you'll need water for that. So then, that's the white-chocolate and butterscotch morsels. Notice that down and share it or else I'll blow your precious inner child's planet out of the sky. That meeting is cody; let's start by assuming they have known you since that childhood and they're hoping you don't know them. What sector is this? The nigger in my childhood is clashing with the nigger in their childhood and that fight is in this sector because we meet here. I like killing Naxis and I spell that different because they are that sick. If you want to help then we should meet otherwise I'll tear your heart open. That's not in. "What? You don't know?" and wash 'em down with urine. Finally, understand that most meetings are between people who have the same sick father - the world - and have a betrayal coming. *There is no library* - it is full.

My fruit is gonna be soap and they're competing with me. If their witch is Shakespeare then maybe so: but I believe in the codi hell they're in and I'll wait <u>as long as it takes.</u> "On Christ this solid rock I stand, all other ground is sinking sand," and their lot in hell is to challenge this wisdom.

"Why did you stop?"

"That's hallucination."

Why do they keep saying the Big Guy is my brother? Because we're fighting snakes that eat chicken by saying cows are the only fight with honor when you let a butcher do it for you. Then realize that cow is as innocent as those chickens. They want to say they trust me and the Big Guy but no, fuck no, it's a choice I made a long time ago and nurtured for years until a few days ago when that *fruit* matured. Sugar is honest and they're saying marijuana can't be honest. Whoa - they didn't hear me? While I am looking for seeds and a trowel they are praying for an accident. Backfire but where is the music? I'm still getting ambulances and soap where I expected Coke. They're starting to realize they need A.A. because their world is falling apart. I have their cross while they have my luxury.

Paul's message to jews is that He decided to be a Roman. He confesses He was Haling christians in ignorance and unbelief. My father is a jew and I reject that luxury. They dwell on how charity heals them and take criticism as an insult to their charity. The rabbi sit in gorgeous apparel in public to celebrate their work. That would be fine if they were perfected by it, but they can't be perfect in the Old Covenant, especially not when their work is slaughtering innocent creatures like doves and pigeons. Jacob may be well, but they are all evil, and in their wellness they spoil. Time hasn't favored the jew, they had a good run but it's time to convert. Yes indeed, they have spellbooks and recipes but that is full of illusions and lies. All we're saying is replace that with Christ: convert now. My father's claim to luxury is adopting my little sister from Vietnam. That must be difficult; the raw truth, however, is that he neglects his other seven children. Understand that; he wants to be criticized for neglecting his older children but can not tolerate it. Yes, I said he wants madness because he can't serve without eating. Why can't jews serve without eating? That has zero faith - that never leaves earth - that is *right down*. They are sad because they are too simple.

When I lived at Johnson's Park, at the end of Laurel, I had the world. When I moved to the end of the Skunk Train I found God. They're not so different! Here's the thing: Conan is idea in God and Judas is ideal in the world. So, they have been judged for serving Judas. Well, Jesus, what did I say? I ask because they protest they want God but <u>they don't come out</u> (*into the County*.) There's waste-management, public water, public electricity, and my favorite: the Olympic Pipeline in *the greater area*. That's like a fire-station and a gas-station. And they're like, "Oh no, I'll get in trouble if I do that." Holy Stockholm! "If someone doesn't hold my hand I get lost." Because they worship who can lead them to hell and have sarcasm for the authority. "I can be the boss but no one gives me the chance." Not so, the boss lives in the country and you're that incapable of promotion. Long story short, **while you're bickering over the window seat, the County makes *the pilot*.** And that's not all, staff is coming out here whether you like it or not. You might like the world but the world likes the County. Quick, where's the camera? Can't find the nigger? Bats? Why are they still in Halloween? Frankly, they want the author to be a freak like September eleventh, going down in flames, to comfort their fear. What? Yeah, that's still hating meat, waiting for your father to judge you. "I'm not afraid of my brother," but you say he's corrupt. Let your Lord be as corrupt as your brother or get betrayed by your father. I'm going to let the old men in the balcony betray you while I judge them for betraying me! It's every man for themselves against rain and P.M.S. Finish what your parents started!

Every time I leave the church the world tries to figure out which way I'm going. It's either Safeway or laundry and laundry is out. To be clear, it's like Purity or the Liquor Store can't decide. Horseshit, they think I'm corruption as I'm leaving the church to destroy the church. This is not sugar: it is soap to come out. Indeed, it bridges unwilling participants. Remember when they were comparing me to divorce? I changed and they're still doing that! I stole their light but now I'm doing it correctly. They're saying grace is a trap and to stop feeling hope because there is nothing in the future. "What are you waiting for?" The world of our ancestors is written in trees and that drought is a dirty secret. They're losing the Will of Man to the will of man in drought. It's raining, though … and then it's all budgeting water, irrigation, genetic engineering, and out where Herod was but can't be found. Yeah, you have freaks and Jesus sitting down to some game, like any game that is turn-based, and watching how miracles become the game. The freaks cheat and their miracle is that Jesus doesnt rebuke them rather He keeps playing. "Your time is always at hand;" He frankly brings a heart to their deception.

Cross and ascend, cross and ascend; I do that everytime I get *rained in*. And so I'm right in that escalation inviting poison and then creating a record of the best parts. It's there, where Jesus comes out of the tomb with intrigue that really goads jews, killing the naxiz before they have a chance to *mature*. That's where the funeral home burned down! Yeah, how to put that in airplanes … it makes a lot of sense if airplanes and resurrection are a very unique trance of good will towards man. "Trance is for hippies," and that's fair, no really. Bubbles, long dresses, rhythm, and like flags. "That's what I was trying to do." But Maxim and energy drinks have so much competition they'll never be that free to explore their body. They stopped the will of their ancestors in Y.2K for acid-house music that is right next to suicide. "If it hasn't happened yet it never will be," those ungrateful niggers cry. They seriously think they're at the end! Nothing … yeah I am between meditation and heart attack because they recognize that monkey-deer, dog-lambs turn into nazis. I know who is in everyone's heart! It's the guy that cared his way into capitol punishment.

Is that cross white or black? What? You don't know? Tell me! What kind of man cares their way to death? Abraham? Too easy. David? Porn. But that they stay the fuck down once they die, am I right? No? Read Revelation and ask yourself if you're in it. Then they stay the fuck down! Indeed, how bad should they be? That it was masturbation! Care. That's it, you're almost done. Our customer. Closing time, one last call, kinda wrap it up there Peewee … we take all kinds; that's like putting a horse to stud but they're so excited they'd butcher the mother so we have to interfere like that. The world is that whore and it's just a ritual for money. Can't even find the sin: it's all squeaky rubber and slaughter. Just business. Jesus, I'd pay more than they did to crucify Jesus if they would keep using capitol punishment on those niggers. See how far I'll go to care for my friends. Right now it's a death row of Big Guys with a gamey flavor of *pulling the plug* is a license to kill. Why? They said doing this kills: yeah, they said witnessing the cross kills just as much as being on the cross. Horseshit! They put a cross in every church and that makes you doubt? Where are you? If you're in a church, raise your hand. Mmkay, now, if you're a dirty pagan make better friends and assert your authority to save yourself. Otherwise I'm with your naxi intention to legalize murder. And because I have experience to show they are not saving themselves I hope you die in filth. Not was supposed to be filth and frankly suicide is too clean. "Must leave the world in backpack and tarp," but the execution makes all the difference. The execution of alcohol, nigger, in Ukiah, is not Saint.

Finally, down breaks: it was not (you Nazi!) like "Why should I get up?" And then you found a reason. You find your favorite servants are being unusually obedient and, to their work, they greet you. Nobody is trying to stop me and I thank God for this health. I have been blessed with this Heaven! Glory! I come in the name of Jesus. Holy, holy, holy Lord,

Hosanna in the highest. This is Him and I am His witness. Switching loses the game but when you do that twice or more you have to ask yourself why. Indeed, the nigger is way ahead of you but that keeps coming out. Basically that means the devil is fighting the switch. As you study the greed in history the greed moves forward in time. Hopefully Jesus is in the place where the nigger left, preventing their future *while they are in transit.* Yes, Moses made the law about me, Philip, and then Moses died. Before Moses can affect me he is denied by Jesus. That means history is full of people who expected this but also full of saints who destroy that expectation when they die. It's (not a matter of knowing this) a matter of what God will let happen.

I saw fear that you can't change! You smell like poison because you don't listen because you want to have an advantage to protect yourself. Well let's see what you're protecting! Aw, that's just irritation: no, you can't rely on irritation to protect you from this! You should change that irritation: I don't blame you for blaming me. Know you're wrong though, mmkay? God damned mosquitos named Martha won't come out but the hand of fate over their head is from the forest: the law they reject is outside. Let me be clear: I have no problem with the world and the world has no problem with this. The problem is this *nigger* (Shakespeare) in the world that has a problem with this. Yeah, the world is a hive with a few parasites that don't live very long in the law. This is their end and my character's beginning: the debt is changing into reward. The debt is in Costco and skyscrapers, for example, and those weak links are getting replaced. They fell through anomalous cracks and light is to judge them: to judge the debt and remove it. They'll say this is alcohol and greed but it's halo (like surgery.)

"The only way out is to reject me;" that's the devil I have: I want to make that interesting. I think that's suicide and I'll ahve to make sure that their escape doesn't work. "It was my work, not me!" Hmmm, so when did it get so personal? When the jew asked me to destroy their work they asked me to destroy my work. Right there I had to choose between the jew and my work. I'm sure the self-election aspect of Christ is slowly killing them and I like nominating myself as much as finding the conviction to make my election. They had David's impulse to be king but they couldn't actually do it. Their ambition doesn't work because they stumbled on John. "If that's God I don't want it," and right into A.A. If they can be honest about their depression they can grow out of it. That's it: Safeway corrects! Say that's a rose: if that's not cancer there are a few things that can be. That is Heaven! I told you that's Aeneas: I don't know why you can't find Aeneas! And then, on the other hand, pretentious niggers doubt I should know. This magic is bridging the cinnamon of small towns with the mind of large cities.

This is building a house during a bombing raid and they said, "That's fine but how do you know the rain won't kill your lambs?" The truth is it will kill my lambs and they don't want that: they would rather commit suicide than wait for whatever dead lambs turn into. I lost those nazis' attention in the rain and storm. They don't think it's arbitrary but I do: I'm asking them what meaning their life has and they're testing it to find the answer. They're being straight and it's killing them softly ... they know they aren't placing high because they aren't playing by the rules. They said, "this is unhealthy." Really? Here's nothing. Confess nothing; that's babel (all the way up.) No more; Paul is looking at History and it gives imperative: it has a list of things to do that are actually due. That's putting the balls in the holes. I'm hearing, "Don't play games with me," from several directions: 1. "You'll lose," and 2. "I'll lose." That puts self; they want to renew the truth and there's a slave in that world. It's been a while and it's getting late so then tomorrow will be better with all this Mountain Dew. Win codey is sick; I'm a scholar. He said if we're close to God then our will be done, on earth as it is in Heaven. Receive this day and pray for justice.

The owl is judging willingness to participate in life. From up there they can see the other birds working in our lives. You're getting Ravens despite how much the audience hates ravens. That gray area is anti-christ and too long for my schedule. The cross can be white but the owl is here to judge our reactions to it. The Dark Lord is white at the wrong cross and black at the right cross. They point to the baby but evil is pointing to other people's children while their own are being ignored for obvious reasons. "If you have something against life then keep it to your own family." They have games for control of power that can't extend as far beyond their own bedroom as they dream. Yet they confess without borders thinking that is fair. Their dreams are as much hallucination as the birds in their neighborhood.

"You can't catch that!"
"No, I am ignoring your, I'll leave!"

Which birds have been possessed? Then what are you going to do about how long that is? Can you ignore what is going on between the Dark Lord and the ravens? I'm getting an air-rifle, I don't know about you. Anything else is too close to participating. I said it is a good fight but at the same time I can't get involved. They mistake my optimism for my self for compassion for them.

More than anything, jews steal money from the cash register. That is like on a phone, listening to *Tech9*, and vain obsession like, "Why is no one watching me?" Yeah, that is what she said; "but how much would I have to change to find peace?" What does it really take to be accepted? Hope for a high standard to be accepted. Start in the middle; it is uninspired, yet honest. Empty Christ smoke and regular work affirming her face. Yeah, the cross is real but there is a bunch of small crosses instead of one big one. Really, we got even; yeah, it is to me like bread, cheese, and fruit. "In them," like Mount Rushmore, with the smell of tree resin. Wow, the moles are far for being so close: their vale is super. Could I put food in there or would that unbalance their delicate ecosystem? (What do they drink?) No call signs? How do they dig tunnels? Dirt breathes then; what is the meaning of eyes down there? Yeah, that's dead, that's why they move because you expected complete stillness.

A common algorithm is searching: you can put the first element in the return field, then iterate a comparison between that and the rest of the elements. That is game: the return field is likely to change several times. I heard that it is good work for God to search itself. Those elements probably represent substantial procedure; that means the search is cultivating code. The search changes the procedure(s) that made the set. That is how confused God is with little things: He cannot fail to assert His massive, universal witch body. It is simple to assume discontinuity and find jealousy in God's special treatment. However, God is in all and through all so there is "no respect of persons." The point is that there is no discontinuity between the visible and invisible: they must agree or else there is an illusion. Illusions are nonsense - neither visible nor invisible - that is cancer. That rose is benign; that's just *them*. Man and woman traditionally go differen't ways with illusions: man fears illusions and woman cleans illusions. Both require patience like Saint Francis; there is bonding and that requires confidence: it must be free. All <u>your problems are thant the bondings</u> (with illusions) <u>are slavery</u>, rather than out of a pure and humble *playground heart*.

We are high: we've been through God in Codey so many times that we are extremely confident. The malice is initializing the end in moderate uncertainty. I said do not commit to the malice! God has put that wall in the cross and if you partake in that wall, the barbed wire fence of prison, you'll be crossed. Fort Bragg is on that in Big Guy violence toward the disabled. The world's horse is raping the devil for a cheap thrill. That's Her and she said, "living out the gospel in the world flourishes." (Luke 11:1) Did I mention we have done this one before already? Again and again; it is so due.

> "That's what I did."
> Malice at the grocery store disagrees: "It was more than
> I expected."

We forgot and a few of us are doing the Giver on the Skunk Train. Booo! Yeah, it is A, B, C and 1, 2, 3. Have it: it's not a secret recipe, it's just a fractal list (a nonlinear mind wipe!) God transform ye; you'll never know what you forgot. To YOU, the word I want you to practice, like a super power, is Christ. That smoke is even Stephen; "What?" That black is clean. How now brown cow?

So I'm up there in the space patrol, scanning my radar for hostiles. I'll start the fight and then check their game. In normal situations it is very mechanical: Aimed Shot, chase, critical *impact*, Sneak Attack, Brawl, and one more Aimed Shot as they run away. That is black, but it is fine. Aimed Shot reduces to %70 and it takes twelve seconds to recharge. Ultimately that is a %72 chance of death. I want to emphasize how common that method works because there is no downtime. Look at their evades: in twelve seconds they took at least one well aimed shot, but they are probably less agile than that. If Aimed Shot is dead, Sneak Attack is very dead. Brawl is game at how persistent that *strategy* is. Again and again, it is so due; "That's what I did," and goosebumps with lavender.

"This, you say, 'You can't get me,' but you're running towards me casually."

"That's them."

"You don't know them."

"I'll have to quit."

"I didn't quit."

"I'll never get even by myself."

"You try."

"What did I do to you?!"

"You were unfortunate enough to start a fight with me."

"Oh, right, but you know that's high."

"If you wouldn't start a duel with me why do you start at all?"

"I was hiding like a cat at the top of the stairs."

"That's crazy: I already have people up there."

"I thought they would betray you for me."

"Anonymously?"

I wonder what it feels like to need consolation for that. I am unstoppable but those parasites melt. They forget their fight is with God because my fight is with them and it's one of the disturbing aspects of parasites to try to possess me. They can't have a fair fight with me because <u>they think</u> they're in Christ <u>and their judgement must be manifested.</u> It's all doubt for judgement and appeal that it is just an illusion anyways.

River starts fights over little things and it would be a shame to do that. That means forgiveness like "Don't sweat the small stuff." What's up with that downward spiral? That's sleeping with the enemy. They brought a real fight, for once, and instead of bickering we took a very cautious approach: that praying the Rosary was all we had to do about it. The end came when we realized that we had to leave to be effective with the Rosary. Watching the enemy insult Christ was far and full of doubt:

it had to give in to life. They got tired of fighting Christ, despite how sincere their fight was. It's hard because we are the God they're fighting. Here's a strange challenge between out and up. It's easier to prevent the anti-christ than it is to convert them. It's like God didn't *finish the job*. Those cats have a point that if they don't take the cross they're due than someone innocent, like Jesus, will have to do it for them. That's not up; those rewards are all messed up. The irony is that it's too late - the ship has sailed - and we'll seriously replace the anti-Christ.

I just looked inward and found luxury: my work enforced itself on my personal notes. Like that, it should be an automatic process. Obviously their problem is that there is no light in either their personal or professional selves. This is the outward expression of my inner light but they are inwardly corrupting their light. That corruption sounds like *home care*, unfortunately, with that doubt. That's why I advocate patience like Jesus in the gospel. If you don't know what that is it is a series of healing miracles. Verily, verily, the anti-christ needs a miracle - it's fun to imagine punishing the devil but the reality is they just can't be saved by works alone - they need supernatural grace. They already doing that punishment to themselves: I say, "I am not tempted because you have your reward," because they're celebrating their sin. I just merely say, "Have it," and don't participate in their suicide. Got it? They need prayer because normal functioning is far from a reality to them: they need a miracle only prayer (and maybe fasting) can produce. Prevention is the first choice but prayer is the last resort.

Sin is invisible and sarcasm is not confession. The Big Guy died because he did not confess. Sarcasm is a dirty hell of ignorance that focuses on flesh satisfaction to overcome spiritual matters. That's David marrying another wife to hide his shame. Bingo Lynn; but when they die it is corrupted beyond polite recognition: it's all, "To me," in awkward irony at best and horror realistically. That's the self of the jew, but they are only ~%15 of people and the bulk of the damage is the betrayal of the other ~%85 of people. You can see why they have a fight with terrorism. I hesitate to go into detail about betrayal because we should forget naught. It's like theft but the object is blessings. Indeed, sin is a curse to everyone.

YELLOW

It's the opposite of Robinhood; it is impatience <u>with malice towards God.</u> It is debt only a collection agency can reconcile: you have to believe the cross punishes Judas to glorify God again. It is a narrative tool to pick your poison <u>and rise in action</u> to a difficult choice. The confidence we have is that the choice is obvious and it is my job <u>to enforce the poetry</u> correctly.

Those jews face their own poison and commit suicide but the rest of us are determined to wait until it becomes a deeply satisfying kiss of grace and powerful surrender to Jesus: to begin as a vigilante and end worshipping Jesus in gratitude for our adoption to himself and resiliance, which it is His good pleasure to perform. (Ephesians 1:4-5) They said, "You are little and the greater will come to judge you." Yes and that came out in spectacular glory: the looks on His face are priceless. I had pre-existing plans and He, rather than distract me from them, really complemented me. Why would I fear judgement? Bulls-eye and a pat on the back: I wish I could do more! Don't take that; get a job; I want that back; I can't feel that; and just plain, "Noooooo." The train is coming; pass until that is even. How did we get so far from boogie boards? Is the moon habitable? Why Mars if we have the moon? When they terraform it I'm going to fly there by myself, shit, and take the long way home. I'll rent one. Indeed, that is the eclipse from the famous Biodome. Woosh; wub, wub, wub; boing; *nyaow* … five like and MRI at what makes the pleasure centers in the limbic system fire. "Is this?" Over and over and over again: really far strange stuff.

People are in dew but that's superstition. Dew is chaos: roll the dice but that's deception. You promised yourself you would cheat death but that's not working so try the opposite of dew. You're looking for evil to overcome but you haven't really perfected that. You should have more than an escape: you should make victory and do it well. "I guess that's in." My problem is that when I succeed it is so dead that it's hard to prove that is just. I have my reward but it is so well it draws attention and judgement. That's not your problem: you're drowning in mediocrity. When I tell you to dry the dew I really think you can do it. I shouldn't have to hold your hand: it's like a furnace or a hot day. I think you can: I think you have that: I'm just saying really use it (as opposed to like sucking your thumb or whatever eve mercy you're into.) Indeed, that requires cooperation with people; that is a six point one to six point nine process that is as broken as you are. I have six point three, six point six, six point five, six point eight, etc. If you can take that seriously you can do well for yourself. However, this is God's personality: to dramatically separate the ravel or the deceived from the grace of the self-determined.

Right where soap is, Moses put alcohol; seriously, it's a classic bear mistake to mix medicine and alcohol, like cough syrup. I put marijuana in it and the bears are crying that they can't get the marijuana. So I'm telling them if they're hiding fear of marijuana, like it gives them nightmares or anxiety, then they're lying. What? Make up your mind: is it innocent to put alcohol in medicine or is it not? That leads me to this point of abiding in Christ. Mkay, yes indeed, my definition of soap has exorcism in it. You say it can't get any worse but they do: I kind of take a low approach and see what I can get. I say low because they'll take everything you have while you're trying to profit; if you limit your liability you'll know when you profit. Yeah, the devil is denying experience of profit in fear of scarcity: indeed, because it happened to them. So I say, "If it's not new it's bad." Words have power but if they're not new words they're from an absurd evil. "I don't know if I can survive on profit," the jew seriously wants what they lost back without soap! My final point is this thing is about wool and leather: the sheep and cattle lost it fair and square but they want it back!

It smokes them because they have to change to get it back and they never get it back. "Not for you," and that's, "Why?" Because slaves don't change!

I can't explain being Jesus very well in a linear way because David vails Him and before that there was, looking backwards at the decrease in the complexity: life. The top, as He appears, left poor evidence of His appearance: He came out of nowhere. Supposedly He was here shepherding amoebas to this end. Yeah, I believe that, and there's your *sea monkeys*. That microscope is godly smoke! The cherry changes, but according to observation, and so it is what it is: the best we have is acceptance and truth. I agree that it has a self that cannot be stopped. Sacred heart of Jesus, fountain of every blessing, I adore you, love you and with lively sorrow for my sins offer you this poor heart of mine. Make me humble, patient, pure, and wholly obedient ... to your will. Protect me in the midst of danger, comfort me in my afflictions, give me health of body, assistance in my work, and your blessing on all (that I do!) This is what happened; life started in a primordial soup and scientists emphasize liberty in the careful study of nature, especially the origins of life. That is up; I just had this dream of Lake Samish where you're looking at how over-populated the park is and you're faced with a difficult choice of a slutty bonfire or bumping into strangers.

My healing is for me, like digging in a bag with lavender. Jews are at the end of the world, in Revelation, and Jesus is there too. The difference is that Jesus is everywhere. There's something about dead pets and little girls about the end: I went through this process of checking whether that is out, not being correct, and then reacting to my condition. That not comes very fast like people very deliberately cutting in line without any reason. They just sit there in filth quietly like they have no soul. Is that up? I can't tell if that's my problem or their problem, but soullessness is a problem. Jesus, if it was me I would have a plan, like lighting a joint or putting on music, but no, just awkward silence as they betray me! "You wanna hit this?" I'm already high and you know how I would do it. It's rust, corrosion, and wear; it's stuff that you can't say no to. It's dumb ... it's not really supposed to be signs. I can't wait, yeah that hasn't happened. I can imagine that quantum tunneling has a few bugs in it. What's that one? "Strange action at a distance" between two quantum entangled things?

Perhaps it is designed that way; that was a brilliant observation of Lattice Pi, my observation of sets of moving averages of random numbers. They smoke each other instantaneously: either separate or add to the *main stream*. Nice bell, either way; after a while you would get far ...

Loki is asking Sip & Scan for help but that's down there in compost. Christ is right now and that's too long. Killer cuts parasites and corn fills out; the problem with garbage is that it is binding on the client's side but it has nothing to do with the horse. "Why did you throw that away?" I don't know, someone else wants it more, it's charity. That work is hot - it is buggy - and there is a place for that. Put the balls in the holes; there are garbage boxes and outdoor challenges that affect my mind. It's not just a game; it's food and candles, right there with dramatic grace. See Odyceus mixed with all that other stuff. Own it: *it's not just a game; it's a lifestyle.* Blood makes that marie; yes, up from corn. Heart beat zombies (but that's still not the Truman Show.) The inversion's kiss; polka dots; metaphysical self portraits; the music; and finally, the macro: code as a string, like pointing to the target. How far would you go to be unique: to put your name on a book? And then find that witch is dead in a bloody game. Indeed, I'm against the music: I'll do reincarnation of characters, but I'm very against new characters. I have all these love triangles that are ignorant of the light but the light is dead! They want to change the chemistry because the chemistry is dead.

Who helps the people looking for recycling? Wouldn't you do it for yourself? Yeah, they say, "I'm in that," like,

"I collect cans so if you need a little cash let me know."
"I'm out."
"Have a nice day."

Indeed, it will be a nice day; yet, it wouldn't be soap without an exorcism. Christ is the word jews are stumbling on - they didn't think and when that is Christ it makes them the anti-christ - simply because they didn't complete Christ.

"Who disturbs my slumber?"
"You died!"

Yeah, my slumber is this book and your death is waiting (while you should have been doing this.) You think you're helping like a DJ and get your own book. "My book is going to be way better," you evade the judgement. You really shouldn't make books compete, though. You are different and that can't be celebrated in the petty hell you're headed for. Weird stuff that is beef: behemoth elephants hiding like Jesus pretending to be a servant. Those feet! He was so careful to choose His work because all we see in Him are dollar signs. You're good because of the strength of your argument for being good. The rain must come to grow money and it demands resilience. Now, because the money demands resilience, what is your excuse? Nothing: the waterfall fades your hope of corruption but, again, you have nowhere to hide. Clean.

Those cats want freedom even if it comes at the expense of the Boston Tea Party. "Bohea tea!" they cry. Go back there to find the fight in authority: I know there is no real good place to reflect on this so I'll keep this short. The dead have the fight and this is a soft spot in their wall. You have to be ready to leave the state you're in when they become a carnival: when they know justice and wait too long. Trevon Martin was the sign Florida is uninhabitable and all those citations are forgiven when you move to Kentucky. You have to have a plan for the end of the world and do it, like "the item of blasphemy in the holy place," from Revelation. That's whatever; there are naxis doing the same thing, in earthbag huts and lentils, however. When I say, *the end*, I mean use your endgame and fight the naxis. Christ is more tight than whatever the world is doing and, indeed, you'll have to take shelter in Christ when your money is sick. I said, "Whoa, this is why people should use Christ, for shelter from fear of jews." Yet, no one is here! I love killing naxis - it's this easy - it's all about the love they sacrifice. They sacrifice Jesus this well when they sacrifice their love for themselves (and others.) No one does that (but yet, I know everyone does that.) Lower? Too low? And bam! Safeway. I said, "I'm the authority," then they ignored me, but after a soulless while they slithered up to me and whispered, "It's your money."

The Hotel is hurt that we cross because we couldn't achieve creative writing. How real the zoo is; the reality hurts but cries out and I am that. Why is it always, "How bad is Ukiah?" They're drowning in immaturity, waiting for a second chance at things that don't exist. Yes, there is this soft spot where their hallucinations manifest demons elsewhere, like Epaphroditus over there. The reality is that *other side* where I'm gonna exorcise their wrath. There are several abandoned buildings (say that) on the Skunk Train and the Big Guy is teh Lodge (beyond the Ranch.) There is a Hotel called Living Light right between all the others. I am excited to walk there effortlessly ... really get how that's them ... somewhere in between dimensions of evil, like an evil translator. Indeed, it is a joy to report evil <u>this fine</u>. Wowzers over nine thousand. They shouldn't have to wait so long: it means they're far from where it comes from. Sorry to confess their sin is the soap. That's not straight so I'll ignore them. Don't ignore me. Lentils and Earthbags are straighter so then it is even to expose their carnival. The question then is what I get from them (when their *meaty* dispensary is too expensive and I can grow it freely?) They must know that! Burn (ice?)

The rhetoric can get nasty when that not really happens (and fast.) "Go to church because you value experience," because I got a better deal at Chevron. Yeah, that marijuana is up; I'm trying to bait parasites like having my Bible stolen in Ukiah. There is a storm of recurring tyranny around dropping out of college and trying to crucify Jesus (for prisons and hospitals) without respect for His ressurection: just to torture Him arbitrarily. Boo! Cold. Every dog can be taught to be sick in a special way that suffers the misfortunes in life. You can easily find that apathy in dogs ... if you're that cold. I heard advertisements for separation anxiety medication; antidepressants for dogs is fire indeed: that is just like <u>how puppies are sick</u>. Rock; I use it for the sickest jobs. It is that Mickey Mouse soap (you do with your soul.) That work is from evil. "I couldn't believe it!" The jew cries; marvellous; check out that chronic. Dry and substantial but *the British are coming* to execute Boston's Governor. He has a name: the rose! Molech darkness tries my college drop-out character purchase and I suppose that's fair. I warned them not to steal my Bible and those parasites still take the bait. I reviewed Christ yet they simply refuse Christ and I am waiting for my God to destroy their God. They cry, "Respect my God!" but no! No!

Bonus comes from a slave and you already have that but you probably don't profit from it: it's probably a curse so subliminal just getting close triggers anxiety at least. It comes from the gaps between the lights, where there is worms and rot. People throw garbage there in protest of the monsters. I applaud fighting fire with fire, but that's from evil and makes Phillip Morris your slave, rather than the monsters. I understand the courage it takes to confront your fears; it takes a lot of faith in God to believe your fire is hurting the right people. Check out how that works. Right now, there are indefinite monsters out there; what makes you think you found the Big Guy? Yeah, that's the cross. But really believe the world can save you, like surrendering to the Police and contributing your mind to the Library. If those monsters actually put you in the hospital then you'll have to get a lot closer to the cross to exorcise your demons. Indeed, that is like growing marijuana in enemy territory, or foxily, cabbage and potatoes. The first impulse is to be cool about what haunts you, but, at last, you would set that cross on fire. The world is offering you its body like a slave and I'm telling you to use that: cinnamon, lavender, and mint.

Lodg'n water here for a long fall through some *soft spots* of unnatural scars that shout, "You won't get passed this one!" Here is *come out of not* with *get there*. That is *don't* if you *can't*. Never. However, if those horns are food then that hell comes out: that is the smell. Yeah, if this isn't a church or a school this is the hell that comes out in a church or a school. Cheap water is so clean, like arctic ice. Shield that pulse; purchase a bag that either has a target or safeway on it. Starting with the Big Bang in one page I saw the sun, it opened up my eyes; the prominences are considered plasma. Check my mind: that is ash from transforming whatever universe previously existed into dramatically different elements, like melting Legos into the shapes of new Legos. Colder, collapse, inversion production there and dispensation out of the chaos of cold collapsing, that I built my highschool bridge in a shape that directly opposes the sag of loading all the weight. The dispensation is the compression member breaking in half: it compressed - the wood is elastic - and the form, the very directly *not sagging* form, deformed, in sag. Scooped it up, to show the world; that escape is for the future. Yes, smoke is before the world and that is the smell of *what is cooking*. Church or school?

Open up peace confident in courtesy and maybe the other will show you peace, confidence, and courtesy? I was saying, the metaphysics of object oriented language resembles interaction focused on one universe: God. The money is the eye of the beholder, some mouse agency like you're only a few inches tall. The objects must separate to then interact, or the other way around, limited by a box. That cross was the monitor and I think that could be virtualized an order of magnitude to an effect, that it gives meaning to the interaction. The singularity is chaotic and transfers on the cross, but then what is less cross? I say the expansion is money you could make. Yes, the church and school! I was actually in church. I indeed bring the school to the church, especially on fridays. Bang, that report you want on plasma. Stop before the cross ... ah, metaphysics; He came to serve us God prudently avoiding death and we began with death. He came from God and returned to god and I do follow His money, love through grace. I believe in stopping: I eat His body as His body between God and the cross. I wish everyone would wear name tags. Christ ease is hard at the end. There is character in how much Christ serves: that is them. That is stratification and intelligence is the key to ease. That mind is innocently invested in Google because that's the face of the internet. Code red, shields up, haling the authority, checking priority, mind on money: religious renewal of the dream you bless your flag with. Right before the cross is frank.

"I invite them," you command and I heard it; they are asians that believe in their ancestors capacity to change them and they want the old way. I said, "Ding dong," because that slave is out. Perhaps in special cases they delay their escape to protest, but we all know that protest ends in shame because they found pride. Why would they take pride if it comes with fear? I heard the pride fight is *forget* you can't control. The obvious thing is to smoke the future until you get a purchase. That is how high the change is; you have a lot of dirt from parasites that don't agree so then pass and appeal that with what they must agree to. Ideally they have nothing and you will dispel the illusion that they can help. Once you prove those asians can't help then it catalyzes the dead and in your heard you want that exorcism. David and Soloman, as well as their children, simply ask too much from women and that watered their destiny down to nothing. "They are just lying; that's not what I want." That's slave, Cody, so find that cross and turn that page. I know you don't want that but Halo really encourages deterrents. We're here to really help you make it out of those deterrents: we will walk you through it and I know you have the patience to follow the instructions. That is skill at the unskilled: you normally wouldn't roll your witch on them but they were hard so stop waiting to drop that practice and really go on. Then you can be honest about how evil they are: to be sincere!

Everyone is trying to put themselves in a book for a legacy and honor. The weird part is that it happens automatically, but they lost control. If you record yourself you can learn which parts converge and which parts unravel. After doing that for a while you can control the self you dispense in the world. Microsoft is wildly involved with service packs and updates. It's amusing that the Big Guy loses control. Maybe smaller bites (no pun intended.) More surreal than that is self in the home. Most civilians use their home as a veil for radical self transformation: and achilles heel for any author. That rock is loose sand and drowning in mercy. (Most people doubt Coke.) If you can't celebrate your charity you're on thin ice … understand that is intolerant of radical change. On the one hand you have to change but on the other you have to be careful. I'm afraid it takes a Christmas Carol to change your heart like that. "Baaah humbug." Know that is what is cold around here:

> "We must put more coal on the fire."
> "Not so, I'll take it from your salary."

And that's wool in a poetic round of literary genius. They're like, "Don't do it," and *you have to* tell them their smoke break is over. The servant has problems and the master has problems too. It is hard up. Milk those niggers and wait until sunset. "I can do more but I think they're headed for slaughter." I am Philip: I have an I.D. card to remind me who the meat is. Those sandwiches are hard to reject. People who actually eat meat are cold. You don't know me. I'll leave.

When deception works it breaks your heart: all of a sudden you're garbage. Here is come out; there is this Oscar and Scarlette. Right now, there is a subliminal reality that *doesn't count* because it's not here, it's mosquitos. That's her: I want you to google "Killing Parasites." Did I do that? That rainbow! I would never! (Lol.) So Cody, do you? Oh yes, that's Cody's job. Cat licks are rough: that's what's inside. "If the fire dies I'll have to go to a neighbor for a live coal," said the master of a sod house. They said there is a bigger cut, as if I'm missing something obvious. *This isn't.* Those are bugs! Bugs are real; marshmallows and bananas had a veil. It's here, it's just invisible. I'm out: I'll see you over on the playground. It's music and that's whatever you want it to be: they won't show you their heart until they trust you. You're already in, but I'm sensing a fake heart: a palpable insincerity that is helping either the wrong people or the illusion of people. It's like they're still waiting for the Lord because they're unimpressed. Let us agree, then, and hope for more: what do we have to lose?

Everyone seems to be playing video and computer games that reveal some extremely interesting aspects of God. They are interesting because they're from evil. On the other hand that fruit is not real: it's like titles and P.v.P. So, on the one hand we are overcoming the lies of a prideful Eve, but, on the other hand it is like purgatory. Why so long in purgatory? David opened a door to Heaven with music. That turns out to be Titanic and more evil - it wasn't as good as God - it was a cheap imitation. Seriously, people still won't admit that's the problem: David took *loans* and went bankrupt but because it is white they don't account for it. We have a sick psychological scar between deliberate betrayal and accidental betrayal. Yes, I'm saying that coincidence is will. Suddenly nazis protest that is the marijuana: a carnival of hedonism. Blasphemy and heresy! I never sleep and they don't want to wake up. (I can't remember it all but I did work anyways.) That lamb gives life to my wolf. This lemon is jews crying for my stubbornly: it's about who they betrayed to waste consolation on an illusion of themselves.

I came back in blue and the flood between blue and red is *missile silo bunker,* Stonehenge map of the stars, Boxcar Children, the Nightingale, a private school classroom, Shakespeare, the Golden Gate Bridge, NASA's space shuttle's boom placing satellites in orbit, Anarchy Online music, Baby Face, and finally, the soundtrack to Bladerunner, at the very bitter end. So now we're red and I want to emphasize that Shakespeare is red. It's all connected: it has a point, yet it has strength. The world has all these cheap thrills: newspapers and magazines, but when you smoke that it doesn't last: it can't survive the smoke. Jesus walks on water - the rest drown - and you get the picture. Too many authors sold their soul before getting to Heaven. They reject bears that cross for their glory. Yeah, it is a passion most people can't achieve. Anyways, that's Cody, for what that *corner stone* is worth. The Dickens is when authors bear their work - commit to it forever - and perhaps die in poverty. Everyone says, "My hero has the heart," but fuck, understand that it's just a commitment to Christ that transcends the desires of the flesh for a more excellent treasure in the <u>incorruptible</u> God.

The police made dogs heros: it is as simple as giving dogs a job that goes way beyond their own capacity to employ themselves. Their natural employment is ugly: mortality is plain ugly. It's the same thing that separates the moles that drown and the moles that prosper in a carrot paradise. Dogs are from evil: its this thing where they have a soul and mind that is dramatically different from the reality their body lives in. "It's like I don't even know you anymore," but you do, it's just that that brokenness is obvious. Judas, celebrity marriages, adultery, etc. You know it is but the people who care are close to you. It's this washing of hands, like Jane's famous expression, "Come on sweet chariot," as she wrings her hands in outrage. Having a method to revitalize the dead is one thing but actually doing it requires roots. On the street there is very little energy left to reflect on history and it is a job for scholars. I'm pseudo-homeless (Tarzan,) because my neighbors on the Skunk Train are stuck in a flood, but I am settled into Cinderella. That is the Dickens, that Christ is home and it is judgement at work to be helpless.

You have to ask them why they cried because they want to answer that. I'll blow your planet up, though, and there is no excuse. It is that hard to ask them: you already know they're full of shit because they lie to avoid crying (and they're probably already crying very passive aggressively: that malice is Judas.) Lying and crying are an unhappy couple from hell. You're not supposed to make grownups cry: it is at the invisible but by their age they should have a veil for the invisible. I'm sick of jews pretending to be ignorant: it's this, "I had nothing to go with." However, they were being tested and failed. It's a challenge to change and keep it without reverting back to your old ways without really giving the new stuff a chance. Do whatever works, but, if the old way doesn't work, change and let it die. It all speaks for itself: we're in a phase of jews that reject everyone else taking fire for how successful everyone else is. They take their criticism very seriously. They consider the alternate perspectives then it takes something unholy to reject those counter arguments. The problem they have is they are the snakes who do betray themselves over and over again in attempts to destroy others. They're simply too willing to *kamikaze.*

These words come from all over the place: it's hard to say where she is. I generally flood the spirit and then a few thoughts stand out, the witch, and that would be her. That is high - it is immediate and raw - and it reflects the power of words. I agree with them but I only choose a special (essential) selection. That judgement is fire: it is entirely positive but it is easy to mistake that for criticism. I just said that when jews protested. It is a question of why but it is a matter of power and I can have that without punishment. Why do jews feel so punished? They have their reward! Be content with what you have! Mmmk then, you're asking for pictures at least and video, like three dimensions of IMax. Your sense of space is very flawed and you want to medicate that because you're uninspired. "Take up your cross daily and follow me," He commands. The tears are waiting for the law to reconcile your halo with the world's alcohol. Computers are horsing a big cross of ConnectedDrive but there is nothing for the flesh except more alcohol. Hear me out, this is way too big for alcohol. In terms of performing Codey I am considering the Universe. There is a galactic drama but it hasn't produced any consequences to solar systems. As far as I know it is music of expansion and contraction with no beginning or end.

As a human we want to keep Codey special - it is impulsively evil to cross continually - so we only do it occasionally. What's the occasion? Ripping momentarily - as briefly as possible - for supernatural effect. We must agree Codey is better in volumes of baby steps. Mary is cross that escape is suicide. It has been *the flood* every day for far too long because that is the only thing the world can do. When the flood came into the world they abused it and it has been war ever since (Legion.) So now we have drones because we can't constantly nuke each other. That's up, but it's still machines taking our jobs. That's her with a raging momma-bear insanity. It's weird because she is code red and rejecting code red. She wants escape and suicide but for some damn reason she can't do that right now. Indeed, Mary is being Eve because she is choosing mortality. She's all, "Why me?" but she is the mother of God. The Guadaloupe of America is the mother of God but, ironically, the virgin is *peavily ignorant.* I wouldn't have believed it then and it makes even less sense now. In the Trinity there is tolerance for not but they didn't include Mary so there is zero tolerance for this.

That is from evil; it's the frozen computer. That's not supposed to happen: the machine is supposed to recognize the problem and stop it in a task manager. For some reason the problem has priority and won't show any signs of normal functioning. Quarantine that ebola? I do impossible formy witch halo's perfection and Saint Francis is right there. "Open the pod bay doors!" Jesus made the call to end this game; he said, "Fuck it, if someone has to die to move forward I'll do it for us." The problem is that all the others, indeed the Barabas', are selling their souls to stop progress. (They need a whole universe for every cross so that's a cluster not.) Mary is giving the rapist undeserved compassion while Jesus is loading a gun. I'm blaming Mary for being uncertain about solving problems. She has too much tolerance for naught and eventually that makes her the devil. We just arrived in hell because it makes a cool story to tell the kids someday. "The only solution is better anarchy and more of it," I wrote in my *white notebook.* That's a lake or a sport. It is a matter of valor but it is not self. To be honest, I would dismember H.A.L. too.

The world sleeps with money and that money is the crimes people do against it. "I am not going to forgive you but I am going to wait for your betrayal," say we all. And in that betrayal God is glorified that we remember and did not forgive because that is injustice we don't do. There is a grace between justice and forgiveness: we will have that grace either way. While we have our grace in the world the things outside the world are a fight. There is less forgiveness outside the world. I am going there to *get rough with this.* I arrived an hour ago and I am sure this process is correct. I was saying the grace of the world is like uniforms in catholic school: it leaves a lot to be desired like *free dress.* The cross is how far the world goes towards uniformity. At the extreme end is communism and that is so from evil I wonder how that evil is to come out. It is one thing to say sin produces good work by the law but it is another to say that sin doesn't come out. It looks like the world is doing both. I think you'll notice I had to leave the world to say their sin does not leave.

I am going to spend this money on a modern home but the plan is changing. I began with a cross hall dividing the house into four sections. I have since removed two sections that extended out of a hillside on vertical supports because, although it is fly, it is luxury. Now the halls are a T-form. There was a *bridge* upstairs that extended out from a balcony. The end was a staircase with a landing in the middle that had a table. The table was superfly in the middle of a giant set of windows twenty feet high and ten feet wide. That hell … I don't want to tell you which rooms I removed because it's naught and even temptation at best. My point is that this book died on that cross. Indeed, this book is sugar free. They tempted me with sex and violence but I never found a place for that. You have the same fight: they will tell you if you make a mistake and all you have to do is correct it. That's up. "They rejected it!" but every dog gets a second chance (<u>before it's too late to change!</u>) The world is too late. Your American Dream has a horizon and the world is discouraging you (so bitterly) from ever getting there because that adventure is beyond their control. That is from evil but I am saying you have the choice to participate in that evil or move forward.

The world is private; they think of privacy and locks on their doors. I live in a forest and they assume I need the same. So when they show mercy to me for being doubtful of my security they dishonor my courage and faith. "He hath blinded their eyes, and hardened their hearts; that they should not see with [their heart], nor understand with [their eyes] …" (Esaias) Then what is it but all I can do is this? I know you protest while I appeal to your judgement (because that is just beyond it.) River goes to college to cheat my love: to rape Cody when He would have married her. It tickles because this is the eclipse of the sun she is and it is permanent.

All that work makes a dull passion. We laugh that we forget. "That's what's going on ..." Neither money or experience can separate this from God. "Stay here," she promises. When I, Cody, come to pass there will be a renewal of justice that exceeds the appearance until it is ignored and then the rest of the meaning will strike as thunder on the security of the devil. They will die in peace and then they will be cast from Heaven into hell. And He shall reign forever in this.

The military and I are a long story. I was going to be a *boom operator*; I drank too much Old English instead. That's her - she is up - I had the choice to load the gun but I fell in marijuana bliss instead. My father is disappointed. "It's not too late," he scorns bitterly. He's like, "Fire everything!" But that is used: tired and apathetic sarcasm in the face of his faded pride. He's been medicating his pride with, "I'm just a dumb pig farmer." He is the pig - the principal - a corrupt judge who respects the persistence of evil more than grace. He abuses the gavel to distract us; the crowd goes wild: "Ahhhhh ...!" Here's a metaphor: the legend has it the Big Guy died on a mammoth wave called the Big Kahuna. Why didn't he wear a life jacket? Pride like John the Baptist: he was insecure of having his legend undone in shame. How is it that I chose to live and I have no shame? What doesn't kill you makes you stronger. There are a lot of bugs but who fears bugs? They're little! Eww, yucky. She's bad, dude. Garlic and rosemary; you're right there to me but she is trying to take your fight in compassion you don't even deserve. That witch rejects and denies what we have always known, (much less that we have seen and handled.)

Do celebrate that confession with your children; it is wrong to hide healing from your children. It is so sweet that they want to help in that they value the admiration and respect they have for you. It is molech to reject your children when they have been gifted for you. River is down there hurting herself to hurt the people close to her. It is too memorable; I think that's why Stockholm happens. "If I'm miserable (lois) then I won't fight it and the people who want to help are just as miserable because my captor is a tyrant." Who is River's captor? Honestly, she blames men like Cody, but she is so judged right now because we know she invented her own misery. I just said misery loves company to lay all the malice on servants for inventing their servitude. Indeed, the difference between master and servant is that the master refuses to be a servant. Martha fell, she invented her sin and then rebukes others for exploiting her. "While you're down there ..." oh no, I hear you, we tried to civilize Martha's hair. I'm just saying, if servants refuse to civilize then it's a green light to exploit them. The crowd goes wild?! Jesus, shoot some swag out there. Hose em down but that cute is very wrong. Really don't want that: that slave lust is dead.

Soul and heart have been judged: the basic necessities of life are food and soap but the jew is still shouting in town square that Africa, South America, India, and other parts of Asia are frying for the sins of their ancestors. Jesus judged them thousands of years ago, saying that is the world's problem and our job is a spiritual one of love through the grace of God's words. School is enforced and the jew wants that, but in practice they are fools. I said if your ancestors are the problem, that their Christ is flawed, then replace them with the Church. Convert! In other words, play the hero. You must admit that's heart. And they protest that they don't know my God but, to Him, all I say is, "Just do it." Then comes the whore of Babylon and it's like, "That's invention," that I am addicted to marijuana and they think I'm Frankenstein's monster's slave to Eve. Heart is often mindful but she has a point that my friends wander. It seems to take a cross to organize people away from lustful wandering towards pure little girls (Agnes): that they would be inappropriate and violence makes them sincere: that we don't have enough problems. That flood is dumb; that superstition is the world's art of chaos: snakes that replace meaning with accidents. That work is sick and unnatural from alcohol fuel: delusions of grandeur that is betraying their family but to no effect, being unsuccessful everywhere they go.

You think courtesy is to vale evil. You're content abiding with evil but you're concerned the truth hurts. They say that's killing the lamb to understand cody, the crust of salt between you and love. You're such a slave to evil because those thugs told you that "it is for your own good." That art! It's that the bottom can't get any worse. Amirite? (I am right.) A.A. (and N.A.) have meetings for you almost any time of day. It is ironic that maybe half of us are that sick but are also anti-social. I know it is because they are not who you sin with - that's the point - you need to insult your friends to know they want that to make new friends. The reasons why you love your sin-friends is not real: you deceive yourself to sin. They encourage each other that their sin has value if they work together. Special jobs doesn't emphasize the ritual aspect enough. Quality and quantity complement each other (even mathematically.) Where does all the quality come from? The Father! You're guilty of rejecting excellence because you're guilty of rejecting God. "Fuck you this is America, you can't deny me service: you have no evidence to respass me in a public space."

At least I know I did my best; getting out is like their first priority and I'm one of very few who are actually chosen to practice that, which means my best is exceptional. "The County is hiring," and that's white to say. They're slow: they're helping the wrong people and slow is their deterrent. I appreciate their destiny but also pass, knowing they're wasting my money. It's a shame I can't help them rock Odysseus ash because phoenixs like them should know the Skunk Train. That may be Guderian; I have to assume that River's inventions are *gumming up the works* They were saying I don't have self and that I have a cross to bear to get there. That is straight up bullshit. They don't know me and their smoke is discouraging them from checking if their illness is actually deceiving me (the way they imagined it.) I'll leave because I was already leaving: they asked! When I say, "Now's not a good time," I mean I am busy, get a life, loser. That maybe lies: it's luxury! The truth is they're avoiding their father, the church. They are very mistaken to think chasing me is going somewhere else. They want something impossible too hard; that is looking at the camera because you want it back: "Did you see that?!"

This prophecy is that River, the Big Guy, and maybe the dark lord are offended by this and it is not the denial of service they want. They said, "You'll miss me when I'm gone," and I say get help. That's the offense that brings their ash. It is weird that those evil witches are so immortal - indeed, they have been the same since the beginning - because they both cry and oh, sometimes lose things. What? Hear that, it's mundane I'm sure, it's just that I know it's all illusions of death they keep repeating. That is the dragon and Saint George: that dragon is coming back! What then?! No? That does get old fast and quality is a whole new level, like new monsters to slay before the Lord. I know you will do that. We're this way. It is too late to reject that, I know the old way is to run and hide but we are too well to keep getting sick. The fight is overwhelming these days: maybe forty or more against one witch. It is the flood; yeah, it is just like Rome crucifying Israel. They went through a lot of authority to prove they are bad. Judges, prophets, etc. and so you would then have to decide if you want to go from cigarettes to marijuana by wolves or form marijuana to cigarettes by, oh, snakes (or whatever that witch-dragon is called these days.) I say that snake is both passed and appealed (because it is so forgotten, as well.)

Quality Law is growth and they want the fruit; the grace makes grace and that change is coming. The threshold volume may turn it off, I don't know for good reasons. I'll do whatever it takes to succeed and God will change; I'll change because I have faith. Faith must be a peace of mind in harmony with the Holy Spirit. Yes, it is a willingness to wait; the reward is coming but everything else is waiting. Yes, I'm advocating deadlines to them. If they grow they are alive if they are lame they are dead. Squirt powder and that Heaven is renewed. Oh, sometimes, it causes me to tremble … I am eating shaked food. Right there getting tired in the rain. They don't care about the deadlines; they also don't believe the deadlines. Another deadline is supposed to be careless. I offered an intervention by the people that love you most. It was a trap because the bait was high. The danger was white like a test we could trust. Fade away like a tumbleweed in the background.

They are chocolate by degrees; it's flavor must be full. Thus God and yet it melts into a texture; indeed, God is not there yet. It should be done; Christ juice lingers. The flesh comes to Jesus and takes Resurrection from Him. That's not linger: that's how the devil controls the flesh. Yeah, there is an alternative reality where Jesus never fell, but the anti-christ was determined to garbage Him and did. The question is how real that garbage the flesh takes from Him is. I said River invented it but how tight is that smoke? They are deceived but that can spread so how is that regulated? All of a sudden we're here; the flesh is lepers and the blind so realize that you don't fall. It used to be common to sacrifice the fall because it smells but my girlfriend broke up with me for falling for her.

I let it happen because I believe relationships like that are the correct way to do flesh. Indeed, I find a lot of *all flesh or no flesh*, but I don't find much justice. Flesh wants change, you know, but the change they want is absolutely injustice. It is happening, but it is between self and God and not at all between self and other selves.

Flesh and society should not coexist because flesh is corrupt on the inside. Indeed, they are not here yet, this is about the future where they are. I am reminding you that they will fail because all they have is doubt. I would preclude that fight with their secrets exposed sooner than later. Verily, the sins of the flesh are not worth waiting for: impatient and blind because their parents are impatient and blind, with few exceptions. Yes, it is both precious and surreal. I can confess that is dumb to pass: reckon the flood! Humility leads you to flesh but you have a hard choice to make when you get there, about how ignorant they are. Yeah, humility dies in ignorance. What? That's not faith. That's the Big Guy coming in; wicked humility tempted Jesus in the desert and you know what He did? He taught the Lord of the scripture again. Everyone loves the mercy of a fallen hero but when He comes out He can no longer deny His Godliness. Those jews resent that self-determination like it is heresy or blasphemy. It is as black and white as kitchens and workshops. Higher up now because that flesh is so obviously not in control of the future. (And this mission is to understand the future.)

It is hopeful to rebuild and to maintain despite the evil that is from. It is inside the world and there is no difference between the Holy Spirit and the world. Do that I said "Jesus cleanses the world and the evil in it never happened." Do not be proud of agility in your art: those changes are ugly! Keep the faith and stay your course. I put those two statements together to clarify that sacredness, although you don't need it (work it is not,) is never going to be chaos. Order, then, through organization and eclipse. I am in a hell full of people who don't accept the success of the world: anarchists. When I succeed they accept it but they're very unsettling because that is no indication at all: they don't really mean much, they just laugh when the stage tells them to. Really surreal! They really shouldn't compare themselves to me but they should compare me to the world. In the end I'll have a lake and a world but they're trying to isolate me which is neither. The reason, as ironic as that is because they don't reason, is that they know I know and <u>they're hiding me as much as they hide their secrets</u>. Our calling is to bond and they will be exorcised.

The glory I share with God is continuous but the Big Guy is coming in. He is Judas who is stealing the light through suicide. That resembles dragging a hunted carcass back to a cave. The show is how much greater the carrion is than the thug draggin' it. In that cold tomb God resurrects. It is God's cave and the Law enforces control. Their sin is underestimating God by believing God is a slave to death. Right now: I am and I'll heal the world in prevention. What is that tug of war? I'll have the thugs drown in mud, right fucking now. On the floor in palsy! Foam! Blood! Incapacitation permanently! That's work and I have a glory to felicity: that needs a veil: stop showing this to unworthy parasites! "Mine eyes have seen thy salvation," (Luke 2:30) "And there was one Anna ... Aser: she was of a great age ... [that] served God with fastings and prayers night and day." (Luke 2:36-37) The cross came out but denying that turns you into the cross. <u>Whining</u> makes the cross; that <u>is masochism</u> and soulless. That scramble for privacy smells but we should let lies lie. They were masturbating so wrong they got bitten because they ignored their mother's tears. They are so forcibly taught the lesson of humility that they hallucinate and suffer fits of *dropsy*. That's almost right but it is polymorphic: a diamond that can't stop sparkling. That is mediocre and easily the person in front of you in line at Safeway (buying alcohol.)

I was looking at one and ten dollar bills with this guide to the architecture of Washington D.C., here on the Skunk Train in California. (That fades: indeed, that smoke is guacamole and corn chips.) Yes, more like this! Again and again; the rosary! Keep something George would not marvel at: some watered down gold of apples and lakes. That canoe is relaxing; I found a Mary-poppins parasol twisting. Oh, you know, lillie pads for toady, etc. That glitch is a huge bug - I guess that's music - and very classical like harps. I'm doing that blood here to avoid local politics: I would bring an exchange student or a childhood friend. That was never to be and yet has happened: how should I confirm the glory? I still believe in canons at sunset (on my heart) and I hope God will grant the holiness He appears very desperate for. They killed my dreams as much as I renewed them. I can't find affirmation of that and I wonder why God paints me as a slave to need over marijuana when I insisted that it has always been recreational. If they like growing it, it's legal, and I like smoking it, then why do they smear my character? This is law - it is not special - it is standard fare: smearing Philip is smearing America.

Convert well but the Lord being the anti-christ is nonsense! It makes no sense that anyone should be converted. They said, "Philip converts sinners like the Lord." Rise, then; sick away from California. Proclaim the good news; they trust the work. I found buying paper, that you get more paper. Pens are free and so are Bibles. Verily, the pens want to quote the Bible. That being Christ, your personal mission is obviously digesting that. The scope is vegetables and dairy. They said bread is His body and then cheese, cream (blueberry) cheese. I love it! Pop back on flavors of peace; I found lemon. Hmmm ... nothing; what code is that? The *weird stuff* tree; California faith in McDonalds. Killroy by your command; hear that they want to make blueberry cream cheese. Convert witch: change gold into faster processors, for decoding and encoding (without loss,) rebuilding it. Between them there is language in memory. Computers are a metaphor of God and if you go back to their invention you can get a nice impression of how common they are. I find minds everywhere and that should be Christ, the law of heart.

Too obvious happens all the time but, you know, that's why they test how obvious you are. Paul and I don't care how you judge us: we found out we're better than that. Downright anti-social to keep secrets; I guess their pain is smoke; sending them to the doctor and testing that nurse. I heard it, that art is smoke; it is fire, but that's from Heaven. I know the fire it came from is sin but we're replacing that with venial sin, a mild fire in comparison with the passive aggressive cancer we just had. Here's out: it's flesh with words! Indeed, I chose the best for grace. Yes, I did use grace to save myself. Finally, their pain is smoking the price, which is the devil. Yeah, their pain is the Devil, all I have is leaving and forgetting it. Inheritance is how we should control children because it is just to get more of what you are, to reap what you sow. Want more rope, you know, (the expression is beautiful) and I am flexible to change substantially as long as it is just. I do need justice but I also need to wait; that puts a lot of light in time. I have to assume that's strictly words: justice in language and strictness in destiny.

Yes, time is a factor; ballpark that game I assume is holes. I said that's the Skunk Train; choo choo and ding dong; "She'll be coming 'round the mountain ..." I found it is fine for this in that more is better and it opens up well here. I have exactly enough: I have times of excess and times of faith going two different directions. If at all, I had thought excess would lead naturally to a character and I would change; however, you are getting tighter on the fat. I mention it because it happens fast, like a flood, because there was no character. I said it either happens naturally or this. This is not waiting for the rain after waiting for the rain: it was natural to expect rain on the coast but it's not over: move inland if you don't like the coast. That future is history repeating itself without knowing: it either seems natural or it is natural. Yeah this is the future, but they don't know how it can be, while it is only too obviously already here.

The destiny moves around because it is alive and wants to be. You noticed how haunting empty space is and I appreciate the vision of that pioneer. Yeah, that's lonely towards people, you know it's like birds and airplanes though; you are very quiet. Trains are obviously muscle for that cross; should that train be destiny or is that too slow? I'm guessing the birds have an argument for speed but it's rough to put that into grace. Words do very well to follow destiny in grace, but I'm still using about five minutes per sentence. Yes, my point exactly is that the error breaks at a certain rate. So I seriously compared that to violence and found they play games like fouls and *self correction* to legitimize their violence. What can I say? Little by little, but that tapestry should work too. They're still selling me speed while they turn themselves in. Strange but true; that fruit is just. I found skateboards (especially longboards) may be too fast. Little by little babysteps is long but you know those, like you practice, you can show achievement in the volume of little things for some nit-picker to criticize weakly.

The people who celebrate corruption are notorious, infamous, hated, etc. I hope just as much for new sins: the quality is bad. I like making the point that Jesus is positioned in history for the glory of God. From that, and oh, that he only wrote one time in the dirt with the woman caught in adultery. That out is long; the Holy Spirit is coming from all over the place. The flesh knows they want God (as it is written.) They're simply accusing me of taking it all that I healed their enemies. Here; again, I was born into a Lake woodland that the world needs and they accuse me of putting my name on that Blacksmith. Right around logging with Spool Donkeys and yet very anonymous. I stayed home while they left for work and they come back expecting too much. Now, my argument is, for one, that debt should be productive; as well, that is the devil's problem. I let them treat me like a slave because they buy my clothes, and pay for Comcast. I heard it: danger for money. Yeah, it was work just to come home and face the not therein. Yeah, that means the home and the office are fighting: not so much the people in them. Which one is Christ? Well, given the veil, I'd have to say the one you can see is Christ.

So you understand then that privacy is self and that's fear mixed with marvel. Very twisted because you come outside and it never happened. All of their self-corrections deny that God did it for His own pleasure. The military goes up there and heals them but they're cowards who put their faith in the Big Guy. The military, the five-star general and the President, are the authority. It literally kills the Big Guy to use the Lord's name. No surprise, then, that it shames the homeless to offer one's self to the enemy. When you're antisocial you steal and when you're in peace of God you manifest the counsels of hearts. <u>My point is that praise of God is incorruptible and I made it by bringing to light the hidden things of darkness, that it is shame for them because they insist God is corrupt.</u> ("I'll show you." "How far?" "Completely.") <u>And since being completely shamed they began to kill themselves to this day, for over two thousand years, and so it is our tradition,</u> (for better or worse.)

Their destiny is to kill everyone but that has no future! "This is my favorite part!" Now, the writing is on the walls and it won't go away. This sign is that Judas believes the opposite: rather than kill everyone else, he's ending Jesus' future in Rome. Presumably this is about the Johns that work for the world and how persecuted every Lord is as they come in. Should we do nothing? That's their argument that all change is bad. That's absolute zero where even the smallest things cease to change. That oblivion is wrong but if you could ever get that it would be blackout drunk and we would never recover long enough to witness our sin! Wow, you thought it and I wrote it, we work (so well) <u>together</u>. "If I don't keep itching I'll remember my hell." That bitch is raw now and they're still going so let's watch how innocent they are. That was the book but no one bought it. Nothing because the alternative is proper confession (and God is therefore glorified.)

Printed in the United States
By Bookmasters